I AM THE WAY, THE TRUTH, AND THE LIFE

DEIRDRE NEMETH

PflAUM Publishing Group
A division of bayard

Nihil Obstat: Father Yojaneider Garcia
Censor Librorum, Director of the Office of Catechesis and Faith Formation, Diocese of Paterson,
August 15, 2022. Renewed: January 23, 2025.

Imprimatur: ✠ Most Reverend Kevin J. Sweeney
Bishop of Diocese of Paterson, NJ
August 19, 2022 . Renewed: January 23, 2025.

The *Imprimatur* is an official declaration that a book or pamphlet is free from doctrinal or moral error. It is not implied that those who have granted the *Imprimatur* agrees with the contents, opinions, or statements expressed.

Publisher: David Dziena
Editors: Deirdre Nemeth, Lorene Duquin, David Dziena
Cover design: Jeff McCall
Interior design: Cassandra Waung, Jeff McCall

Pflaum Publishing Group, a division of Bayard, Inc.
500 Salisbury St.
Worcester, MA 10609
800-543-4383
pflaum.com
bayard
ISBN 978-0-89837-000-3

PRINTED IN THE UNITED STATES OF AMERICA

FSC www.fsc.org MIX Paper | Supporting responsible forestry FSC® C005010

TABLE OF CONTENTS

A Promising Solution

This book was written for Directors of Faith Formation/Religious Education, Parish Catechetical Leaders, and Pastors. It presents an innovative and promising new Family Faith Formation Program that is successfully taking root in parishes in the Diocese of Paterson, New Jersey. By making Mass the center of religious education, the program moves beyond a sole reliance on the traditional classroom model and enables both parents and their children to learn the faith and live their faith prayerfully and sacramentally.

This program was developed under the invaluable leadership of Father Richard Carton, while Pastor of St. Vincent de Paul Parish in Stirling, NJ, from 2011–2024 and as of 2024, as pastor at Our Lady of the Lake in Sparta, NJ. As a deeply devout and devoted priest, Father Richard has led the charge to explore more effective approaches to help parents take on a greater role as the primary educators of their children's faith. This program would never have developed as it has without his great wisdom, foresight, and courage.

Bishop Arthur J. Serratelli endorsed the program, describing it "*as one of the most successful new approaches of our times.*" Parishes that have implemented the program have enthusiastically endorsed it, noting the transformative power it has had on their parish families (pp. 13–14).

In the new Church's *Directory for Catechesis*, a renewed emphasis is placed on catechesis in the family, with the family and of the family. The *Directory* also emphasizes the integral link between Mass and catechesis. "*The liturgy is one of the essential and indispensable sources of the Church's catechesis, not only because catechesis is able to draw its contents, vocabulary, actions, and words of faith from the liturgy, but above all because the two belong to one another in the very act of believing...* ***liturgy and catechesis are inseparable and nourish one another.***" [1a]

This book presents theological reasonings for and practical advice on incorporating the following three components into the structure of faith formation that appeals to and engages the entire family:

- Catholic spiritual pillars are experienced as a family and church community, including Sunday Mass, Praying the Rosary, Eucharistic Adoration, Confession, Stations of the Cross, and Divine Mercy Sunday.
- Family Faith sessions are attended by families with children of all ages in an interactive faith learning experience.
- Age-level classes for children are centered around the Mass with learning opportunities for parents.

Deirdre Nemeth has been a Director of Faith Formation since 2010 in the Diocese of Paterson, serving for 11 years at St. Vincent de Paul Parish in Stirling NJ and as of 2024, at Our Lady of the Lake in Sparta, NJ. She served on the board of the Catechetical Leaders Association for the Diocese of Paterson as President, Vice President and Member-at-Large. She has earned a certificate in Catholic Evangelization and in 2025, will complete a Masters in Pastoral Ministry at Immaculate Conception Seminary, School of Theology, Seton Hall University. She is a wife and mother of two adult children. She can be reached at MassCenteredFF@gmail.com.

DICASTERO PER L'EVANGELIZZAZIONE

SEZIONE PER LE QUESTIONI FONDAMENTALI
DELL'EVANGELIZZAZIONE NEL MONDO

Il Delegato per la Catechesi

RE: *I Am the Way, the Truth, and the Life—Mass-Centered Family Faith Formation*, by Deirdre Nemeth

The Church Fathers in particular understood catechesis to be closely linked to the liturgy. Cardinal Walter Kasper, a member of the Roman Curia, described "liturgy as sung dogmatics." Perhaps in this vein we can also speak of "catechesis as speaking faith." For only that which takes shape can make a name for itself. They know that the "lex orandi" expresses the "lex credendi." In this sense, what we pray always shows what we believe. Especially regarding catechesis, we can see that not only the *what* but also the *how* is of great importance. How we celebrate therefore determines how and what we can believe. We then speak of the "lex catechizandi."

In the USA, this awareness of catechesis grew earlier than in other local churches internationally. Not least the OCIA (formerly the RCIA) has shown since the Second Vatican Council that the intertwining of phases in learning the faith and confirming and strengthening rites of passage enables a much deeper awareness of faith. It is these experiences, which, starting in the USA, have now also shown in other local churches around the world that the Church's catechesis in its comprehensive form must always be catechumenal. The new World Church *Directory for Catechesis* has further strengthened this profile in continuation of the previous document from 1997.

If in the new *Directory* of 2020 the relationship between kerygma and catechesis is understood precisely in the inspiration of the catechumenate (cf. DC, Art. 57-65), this connection means that the faith has gone through the mind of the catechist to the heart in such a way that he is able to exemplify the whole of the Christian faith in a scriptural pericope or in a liturgical symbolic action. Pope Francis already emphasized the importance of the kerygma for missionary catechesis in his first Apostolic Exhortation (cf. EG, Art. 163-168).

Igniting this dynamic in catechists is the prerequisite for instilling in learners what constitutes lasting enthusiasm and orientation in the faith of the Church. Only when the word leads to celebration do all catechetical learning dimensions come together. Indispensable cognitive and voluntary parts only make faith resound when the liturgy becomes a larger resonating body and thus experiences its affective deepening. In this context, the Fathers of the Church speak of mystagogy, which every true catechesis needs, and understand this to mean guidance into the mysteries.

The first section of the Dicastery for Evangelization is endeavoring, beyond the Holy Year 2025, to support initiatives such as those in the USA, which are exemplary for the universal Church in the practical development of the inner connection between liturgy and catechesis. With this in mind, *I Am the Way, the Truth, and the Life—Mass-Centered Family Faith Formation*, by Deirdre Nemeth, demonstrates and communicates this connection in a practical way. May the catechesis of the Church thus become a real "κατ- εχειν" and bring about the echo of faith in the lives of the learners.

Rome/Vatican City, in the Holy Year 2025.

+ Franz-Peter Tebartz-van Elst

Dr. Franz-Peter Tebartz-van Elst
Curia Bishop
Delegate for Catechesis in the Dicastery for evangelization

DIOCESE OF PATERSON

Diocesan Center
777 Valley Road
Clifton, New Jersey 07013

(973) 777-8818 Fax (973) 777-8976

Office of
THE BISHOP

December 19, 2024

To Whom It May Concern:

"*I Am the Way, the Truth, and the Life*" is a wonderful contribution to the future of catechesis and parish renewal. Deirdre Nemeth has skillfully integrated the principles of family catechesis into a program that is profoundly centered on the Eucharist and fully aligned with the Church's call for evangelization in the 21st century. Her work stands as a beacon for forming disciples and revitalizing the faith of families through intentional and sacramental catechesis.

In this innovative program, Nemeth reclaims the essential connection between catechesis, family, and liturgy, addressing one of the most urgent challenges in parish life today: the disconnect between faith formation programs and active participation in the sacramental life of the Church. By making the Mass the cornerstone of her approach, she offers a transformative framework that invites families into a deeper encounter with Christ and His Church.

The Diocese of Paterson has already witnessed the remarkable fruits of this program. Parishes that have implemented this Mass-centered model report renewed vitality, stronger bonds among parish families, and significant increases in Mass attendance. This program exemplifies the heart of the New Evangelization, inspiring families to live their faith authentically and engage actively in the life of the Church. I strongly recommend it to catechetical leaders, pastors, and all who are dedicated to renewing the Church's mission of evangelization and formation.

Sincerely yours in Christ,

Most Reverend Kevin J. Sweeney, D.D.
Bishop of Paterson

ENDORSEMENTS

Most Reverend Arthur J. Serratelli, STD, SSL, DD

Bishop Emeritus, Diocese of Paterson (Served as Bishop of Paterson, NJ from 2004—2020)

In a time when there are many challenges to the Church's mission of catechesis, it is indeed encouraging to see the creative and fruitful methods that catechists are beginning to use to pass on our Catholic faith. Deirdre Nemeth's approach outlined in this book is one of the most successful new approaches of our times. The home is undoubtedly a privileged place of catechesis. Her approach of family faith formation not only recognizes this reality but helps the parents both grow in their own faith and in their responsibility of bringing up the children in the Catholic faith. Anyone who adopts this method of catechesis cannot help but see positive results."

Father Yojaneider Garcia, *Director, Catechetical Office and Faith Formation*

Diocese of Paterson, New Jersey

Deirdre Nemeth's *I Am the Way, the Truth, and the Life* is a profound and timely response to the Church's call for renewed evangelization and catechesis, as articulated in the 2020 *Directory for Catechesis*. By placing the Eucharist at the heart of faith formation, this program embodies the sacramental core of catechesis, fostering a deep and transformative encounter with Christ. Its family-centered approach further empowers parents to embrace their sacred role as the primary catechists of their children, strengthening faith within the domestic Church. The effectiveness of this model is evident in the revitalization of parishes that have adopted it, with increased engagement, discipleship, and community flourishing. I strongly encourage all catechetical leaders to implement this program in their parishes if they wish to join the catechetical renewal movement that the Holy Spirit is leading today.

Most Reverend James F. Checchio, JCD, MBA

Bishop of Metuchen, NJ

The *I am the Way, the Truth, and the Life Mass-Centered Family Faith Formation* program is a welcome contribution to the parish efforts to orient families to living and learning about the Catholic faith with the Mass and the Eucharist as the focal point.

Father A. Richard Carton,

Pastor, Our Lady of the Lake, Sparta, NJ, as of 2024
St. Vincent de Paul Parish, Stirling, NJ 2011-2024

St. Paul VI wrote in *Evangelli Nuntiandi* (41), "Modern man listens more willingly to witnesses than to teachers, and if he does listen to teachers, it is because they are witnesses." The *Catechism of the Catholic Church* clearly states that parents have responsibility for the education of their children. Of course, the *Catechism* speaks of their education in faith—that is the one aspect of education which serves us to and through eternity. Deirdre Nemeth is a parent, teacher and witness. Drawing from her years of experience and watching the decline in the practice of faith as secular pursuits take center stage, she has compiled a program of family faith formation. In this program parents, who often feel inadequate in teaching the faith, and parish directors of faith formation programs are drawn together to create something beautiful. Children and parents, side-by-side, learning and growing in faith is a beautiful gift for all involved.

This is a gift beyond measure in our ever-changing culture where the faithful person meets challenge after challenge. Deirdre also offers the parish staff, either director or catechist, the opportunity to bring to families aspects of our faith that are essential. She has worked tirelessly to bring together a succinct program, easy to implement and follow, with a depth that is essential for faithful witness. Those who use this program of family faith formation will advance the faith of adults and children preparing them to both teach and witness to Jesus Christ in the living of their lives.

Ministering with Deirdre these past years have allowed me to see firsthand the benefit of this program of catechesis. With change, programs sometimes meet resistance. However, we are aware that the former classroom model that has been used is not effective and it is a Spirit-driven move to try that which is new. May the Holy Spirit allow each to persevere in effective formation not just for a child, but for every family who seeks to know and love Christ more fully.

It Is Not Complicated

The family faith formation (a.k.a. religious education—R.E.) program described in this book, at its core, is about making the Mass and the Eucharist the source and summit of every religious Education program. After all, the *Catechism* states

> **"The Eucharist is the source and summit of the Christian life...the sum and summary of our faith: Our way of thinking is attuned to the Eucharist, and the Eucharist in turn confirms our way of thinking."**
> (CCC #1324 & 1327)[1b]

When families experience the presence of Jesus during Mass, God takes hold of them and enlightens them. Mass, which is Heaven on earth, and Jesus, in all his glorious fullness as Eucharist, must become the heart and center of every family faith formation/religious education program. They will come! It is that simple.

Catechetical leaders do have the keys to the kingdom on earth. They only need to open the door wide by structuring the program with Mass as the primary component. All other aspects of a faith formation program must first flow from Christ. There can be no other way other than "In Him, Through Him and with Him"[2] and no other way is working. The statistics on the fruits of religious education programs, as shown in this book, are telling. *"I am the vine; you are the branches. Whoever remains in me and I in him will bear much fruit, because without me you can do nothing"* (John 15:5).

Originally, religious education was a supplement to the Mass and over the past century, the tide has turned where today going to Mass is viewed as a supplement to religious education. Catholics must return to the Holy Sacrifice of the Mass! Success will be defined by our ability to reverse the thinking of Catholics making God, through Mass attendance, the center of their lives. The chart below demonstrates that U.S. weekly Mass attendance has steadily declined in the last sixty years. Parishes that have implemented this Mass-centered program, in a short time, have already had success in beginning to reverse this trend.

U.S. WEEKLY MASS ATTENDANCE RATES[3]

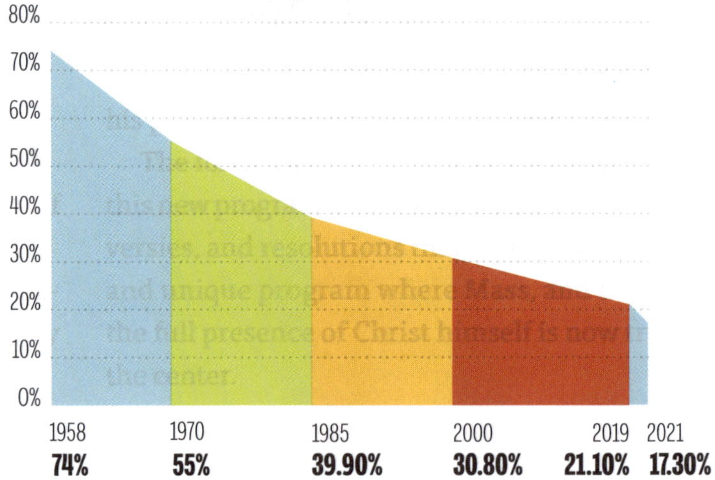

Pope Benedict XVI stated,

"WITHOUT THE EUCHARIST, THE CHURCH SIMPLY DOES NOT EXIST." [4a]

The Old Testament and the New Testament all culminated in Jesus' suffering and Death and Resurrection so that He who is God could give us the greatest intimacy with Himself, the fullness of His divine love and the infinite ocean of His mercy. Through the Mass, God comes to dwell in the deepest recesses of our being! Who could have fathomed that God would enter our very body and soul to become one with us and make us "partakers of the divine nature" (2 Peter 1:4)! It was beyond human comprehension and cost Jesus his very life.

"I am the living bread that came down from heaven; whoever eats this bread will live forever; and the bread that I will give is my flesh for the life of the world. The Jews quarreled among themselves, saying, 'How can this man give us (his) flesh to eat?' Jesus said to them, 'Amen, amen, I say to you, unless you eat the flesh of the Son of Man and drink his blood, you do not have life within you'" –John 6:51-53

As Catholics, we need to look no further than the Holy Sacrifice of the Mass from which almighty God and the infinite treasury of His graces flow into our heart and into the world! It is here that His life and love shine on us and in us brighter than the sun! Catholic programs must reflect this belief.

Parishes should heed the voice of the Church when she expresses the *"Liturgy is the privileged place for catechizing the people of God"* (DC #96). [4b] and that the participation of the faithful in the Eucharist is the primary means of education in the faith (*GDC* #51)[5a]. The new *Directory for Catechesis* goes on to say: "*...Liturgy and catechesis are inseparable and nourish one another*" (DC #96).[5b] Instead of first meeting in a classroom, we must first meet where God lives and reigns; for it is only *"in him we live and move and have our being"* –(Acts 17:28).

1 Introduction

PROPOSED NEW STRUCTURE OF CATHOLIC RELIGIOUS EDUCATION/FAITH FORMATION

In 2011, I attended a national convention on religious education. It was fascinating to learn that directors of religious education from every corner of the United States expressed the exact same concerns. With exasperation, many shared their observations that parents make a commitment to take their children to religious education classes but do not make the same commitment to come to Mass every Sunday.

Unfortunately, U.S. Catholic statistics reveal that a staggering 80% of religious education students, after having received the Sacrament of Confirmation, will abandon their Catholic faith by their early twenties.[6] Parish religious education, in its present state, seems to have little effect on inspiring and leading students and their parents into the fullness of living a sacramental life.

While it may seem a contrary statement, it is precisely because parents are dedicated to the religious education process that religious education programs have the potential to become powerful engines in leading the entire family to Mass and into understanding and embracing all that it means to be Catholic.

Consider this statement from the USCCB on the New Evangelization:

> **The focus of the New Evangelization calls all Catholics to be evangelized and then go forth to evangelize. In a special way, the New Evangelization is focused on 're-proposing' the Gospel to those who have experienced a crisis of faith. Pope Benedict XVI called for the re-proposing of the Gospel "to those regions where the roots of Christianity are deep but who have experienced a serious crisis of faith due to secularization." The New Evangelization invites each Catholic to renew their relationship with Jesus Christ and his Church.**[7a]

Evangelizers are called to graciously and compassionately meet people "where they are at" in this secular culture. In truly loving our neighbor as ourselves, leaders of the Church, such as pastors and religious education directors, must recognize this joyful yet very serious responsibility in making sure no one is left "where they are at" but through every holy effort and prayer lead them on a path to their salvation in Christ.

IMPLEMENTATION OF AND EXPERIENCES AT DIOCESAN PARISHES

> **"The ultimate end of catechesis is communion with Jesus Christ." (DC #426)**[7b]

By revisiting and revamping the current religious education system, a new system has been developed and implemented at St. Vincent de Paul Parish in Stirling, NJ. This family faith-based program, within a short time frame, has been very effective in educating and leading parents and their children to Mass and the Eucharist and additionally to Reconciliation/Confession, the Rosary, Eucharistic Adoration and Stations of the Cross.

This is a multi-faceted program with Mass as the central component. After years of trying to get everyone to come to Mass, we finally made Mass a requirement of the program for both parents and their children and reduced the class time to thirty minutes immediately following Mass. We saw a threefold increase in the amount of times families came to Mass from prior years (from 20-30% to over 90%)! Additionally, because the class time is short, many parents opted to stay and enjoy coffee, snacks, fellowship and/or take advantage of opportunities to learn more about the Catholic faith.

By placing Mass at the center of the faith formation program, we believed many more souls would be brought directly to the presence of Christ whose grace would work on them in ways that the education portion alone could not.

Other parishes in the Paterson Diocese who have implemented this concept have experienced remarkably similar results—a tremendous increase in Mass attendance (some over 90% participation) while the program is in session along with the ability to offer parents fellowship and faith-learning opportunities after the Mass. We are all discovering that within a reasonable program, parents are more open to attending Mass than we previously understood.

What follows are quotes from parishes within the Diocese of Paterson that have recently (2018-2020) incorporated this format with Mass as a requirement followed by a thirty-minute class.

Cathedral of St. John the Baptist

PATERSON, NJ

(as reported in The Beacon 6/13/19)

Ivannia Vega-McTighe, Diocesan Assistant Director of Evangelization

"This program has made a huge impact at St. John's. Families are more enthusiastic about coming to Mass together and sharing their faith at home. They also are building relationships with our priests and each other. We want to give families time to fall in love with the Eucharist—the key to every Catholic's life. Our catechists see our parents as partners—as the most important part of their children's faith formation."

Cathedral of St. John the Baptist

PATERSON, NJ

Rev. Msgr. Geno Sylva, , *S.T.D.*

Rector and Vicar for Special Projects

"The family faith formation program that Ivannia Vega-McTighe instituted here at the Cathedral over four years ago has led to grace upon grace! It continues to be one of, if not the most effective forms of evangelization that I have ever witnessed. Parents begin to experience the power of life-long faith formation which, by God's grace, opens them up to a more active sacramental life. In fact, many of our parents have become our greatest evangelizers, not only bringing others to the weekly reflections but also by volunteering to serve in various ministries here at the Cathedral. More than a program, it is an arena in which parents, children, catechists, and priests/deacons come to know one another, realizing the great joy of being members of the Mystical Body of Christ."

St. Kateri Parish

SPARTA, NJ

Cheryl Wallace, Director of Faith Formation

"As a DRE, I can really see that this model is helping parents and families to practice prioritizing the Lord's Day in their weekly schedule throughout the year, and that it is bringing parents/families to Jesus in the sacraments on a regular basis. I am also elated that this format has significantly increased my parent/catechist volunteers! One parent, who is also a catechist, expressed her enthusiasm for the program at a catechist meeting by sharing how much the children really enjoy seeing their friends and classmates at Mass."

St. Catherine of Siena Parish

MOUNTAIN LAKES, NJ

Rev. Jared J. Brogan, S.T.L., Pastor (2015-2020) Office of Divine Worship (2020-present)

"The implementation of this catechetical format has made a great difference in the lives of our families and parish family as a whole. Catechizing the whole family provides an opportunity for us to be faithful to our universal call to holiness and discipleship; centered around the Eucharist."

St. Catherine of Siena Parish

MOUNTAIN LAKES, NJ

Lisa Gervasio, Director of Religious Education

"The Mass/class format of celebrating the Catholic Mass with families as part of the religious education program puts Christ at the center of the program. The experience of leading parents and their children back to the habit of praising God at Mass allows families to make that connection from the classroom catechesis to Mass. I see this approach strengthening their relationship with Jesus and the Church community."

St. Mary's

DENVILLE, NJ

Father Martin Glynn, Pastor

"St Mary's Parish in Denville began the Mass-centered religious program last year. Since then we have seen a 60 percent increase in Mass attendance among the parents of our religious education children. I firmly believe that the Celebration of Mass has to be the very center of any religious program."

St. Mary's

DENVILLE, NJ

PJ Miller, Director of Religious Education

"As the DRE of a multi-session program, the announcement to the parents of the new routine was met with much resistance. Many did not want to be told what Mass they had to go to or that their Sunday morning routine of going shopping while the children were in CCD had to be altered. Once we were up and running the following are just some of the comments I received from parents:

- *"Thank you for making us return to church. I did not realize how much I missed it."*
- *"While not always convenient, it really has brought a new dimension to our family life."*
- *"Being told I had to go to Mass was not what I wanted but is what I needed."*
- *The general feeling from regular attendees is that "it is nice to see the church so full."*

Not only are the families more conscientious about making the Mass part of their Sunday, but we as a parish are embracing how to make the schedule work to assist the families."

This book presents the Catholic challenges in our religious education programs and very promising and concrete solutions to the most striking question of our times, "How do we get our Catholic families to go to Mass and embrace their faith more fully?"

2 The Mass as Catechesis
IN THE CHURCH'S OWN WORDS

Catechesis is intrinsically linked with the whole of liturgical and sacramental activity, for it is in the sacraments, especially in the Eucharist that Christ Jesus works in fullness for the transformation of human beings. Therefore, liturgy and catechesis are inseparable and nourish one another
(DC #96)[8a]

The Liturgy (Mass) is the privileged place for catechizing the people of God.
(NDC #33)[8b]

Mention must also be made.....above all of the participation of the faithful in the Eucharist, as a primary means of education in the faith.
(GDC #51)[9]

"In the Churches Own Words" is the major addition to this edition of the book and was written to set forth more explicitly, according to Mother Church, the necessary connection between Liturgy (Mass) and catechesis and as such will act as a preface to this Mass-centered program. Beginning this book by first contemplating the Church's own words, catechetical leaders can feel inspired with a renewed sense of responsibility in carrying out the Church's mission of making sure Mass is the heart and center of catechesis. Our religious education programs have not and will not flourish without Christ, who established the Mass as His perpetual presence in and for the world.

Most directors of religious education (DRE) are painfully aware that invitations or instructions to religious education families to attend Mass largely go unheeded. The problem with Mass attendance rates has not been resolved in sixty or more years and continues to deteriorate (statistics, p. 21). While parishes are frustrated by this, most have not recognized or addressed the disconnect between their religious formation program and the Mass. The primary job responsibility of the DRE has typically been educational instruction outside of any liturgical setting or foundation.

As a result of this mindset, it is not surprising that a typical response among DRE's (myself included) when addressing the lack of Mass attendance has been,

"We encourage our families to come to Mass..."

"We make it clear they should come....."

"It is stated in our religious formation pamphlets...."

which is then followed by a headshake and a hand gesture of surrender with a concluding,

"Oh well, other than that there is really nothing we can do."

Catechetical leaders may have succumbed to the fear of losing parishioners by requiring Mass attendance and are therefore hesitant to consider changing from a classroom-based model to a Mass/class family model. However, proper formation in the Catholic faith can only happen when both students and their parents attend Mass, which must become foundational to the program. To allay any doubts, one only needs to consider (in addition to the success demonstrated in parishes with this model) that the most authoritative voice on the importance of directly leading faith formation families to participate in Sunday Mass, is and has been all along, the Church herself. An analysis of the Church directives and teachings on the following catechetical topics will demonstrate the intrinsic relationship to the Liturgy (Mass).

Catechetical-Liturgical Church Directives

A *Directory for Catechesis* (New Edition—DC), The *National Directory for Catechesis* (NDC) and the *General Directory for Catechesis* (GDC)—Liturgy (Mass) is Catechesis

B Parents, Children, and the Mass

C Historical Context of Religious Education and the Mass

D Catechesis and Priests

E Evangelization and the Mass

F *Order of Christian Initiation of Adults* (OCIA)—The Church's "Model of all catechesis"

G Confirmation and the Mass

H Leadership in and through Christ

A DIRECTORY FOR CATECHESIS (DC), THE NATIONAL DIRECTORY FOR CATECHESIS (NDC) AND THE GENERAL DIRECTORY FOR CATECHESIS (GDC) – LITURGY (MASS) IS CATECHESIS

The *DC*, *GDC* and *NDC* provide a strikingly clear and convincing theological foundation, upon which this program is built, for why the Liturgy (Mass) is and must be the primary means of catechesis. The *NDC* begins by acknowledging the cultural shift that has led to an alarmingly low Mass attendance.

- *The way people, including Catholic people, choose to live their lives today simply does not allow them the same free time that they once had. Family and other social commitments are often arranged so that attendance at Mass or participation in catechetical programs becomes very difficult.* (*NDC* #4-C)[10a]

The Church also directly asserts that the Liturgy and Catechesis were never meant to be separate entities:

- The liturgy is one of the essential and indispensable sources of the Church's catechesis, not only because catechesis is able to draw its contents, vocabulary, actions, and words of faith from the liturgy, but above all because the two belong to one another in the very act of believing.....Catechesis therefore cannot be thought of merely as preparation for the sacraments, but must be understood in relationship to liturgical experience. Catechesis is intrinsically linked with the whole of liturgical and sacramental activity, for it is in the sacraments, especially in the Eucharist that Christ Jesus works in fullness for the transformation of human beings. **Therefore, liturgy and catechesis are inseparable and nourish one another.** (*DC* #95, 96)[10b]

- *Catechesis is intrinsically bound to every liturgical and sacramental action.* ***Frequently however, the practice of Catechetics testifies to a weak and fragmentary link with the liturgy.*** (*GDC* #30)[11]

- *In the Church's mission of evangelization, Catechesis and Liturgy are intimately connected. Catechesis is intrinsically linked with the whole of liturgical and sacramental activity....* ***Liturgy itself is inherently catechetical.*** (*NDC* #33)[12]

- *Mention must also be made.....above all of* ***the participation of the faithful in the Eucharist, as a primary means of education in the faith.*** (*GDC* #51)[13]

God is revealed to us in His presence through the Liturgy (Mass) and Eucharist.

- *The history of salvation, from the creation of the world to its redemption and eschatological fulfillment in Jesus Christ is celebrated in the sacraments, especially in the Eucharist. That is why* ***the Liturgy is the privileged place for catechizing the people of God.*** *...... Through the Eucharist, the People of God come to know the Paschal Mystery ever more intimately and experientially.* ***They come not simply to the knowledge of God—they come to know the living God.*** (*NDC* #33)[14]

To get to know a person, one must be with that person. Imagine if children were taught about their parents before meeting and spending time with them. They may learn how wonderful it would be to have a mother or father wrap their loving arms around them, to tuck them in bed at night, to care for them and teach them the ways of life. However, without experiencing this love, over time, they may stop desiring whom they have learned to live without.

Love precedes understanding. From the moment children are born, without the intellectual capacity to comprehend, they are imbued with love's embrace. So important is receiving love first that studies have shown that babies "who are not held, nuzzled, and hugged enough can stop growing and if the situation lasts long enough, even die." This research was conducted in response to high infant mortality rates found in some orphanages.[15]

In an analogous way, God's grace and love precede and strengthen our ability to respond to love. This is why we are baptized with God's mighty and tender love as infants. God knows we must first receive love in order to give love.

And so it is with God's presence at Mass and in the Eucharist. We cannot simply learn about Christ without experiencing Him who enkindles in our hearts a flame of yearning more deeply for God. Religious education programs knowingly are conducted without families attending Mass. The many years invested in solely classroom-based models have indirectly encouraged a continued withering away of a desire to attend and appreciate Mass, and eventually to be Catholic. There can be no doubt that there is a direct relationship between the lack of exposure to Christ's presence in the Mass and the decreased desire to immerse oneself in the true faith.

- ***The definitive aim of catechesis is to put people not only in touch but in communion, in intimacy, with Jesus Christ****; only he can lead us to love the Father in the Spirit and make us share in the life of the Holy Trinity.* (*NDC* #19B)[16]

- As *"the Eucharist is the source and summit of the Christian life"* it makes every sense that *"the first and last point of reference of this catechesis will always be Jesus Christ himself, who is "the way, and the truth, and the life."* (CCC #1324/1698)[17]

The very meaning of catechesis is "the act of handing on the Word of God" and the entire Mass is rooted in Scripture, in God's own words![18] In the three-year cycle of Bible readings at Mass, almost the entire New Testament and all of the critical points of the Old Testament will be heard.[19]

- The *Directory* is replete with passages exemplifying how catechesis only exists in its fullness in the profound symbiotic relationship with the Liturgy. ***The homily occupies a privileged position (of catechesis)*** since it takes up the journey of faith put forward by catechesis and brings it to its natural fulfillment. (*NDC* #34D)

- *Parishes should present catechesis that restores a sense of the sacred and transcendent life.... Encourages believers to encounter Christ frequently in the celebration of the sacraments.* (*NDC* #42E)[20]

B PARENTS, CHILDREN, AND THE MASS

Just as the Mass and catechesis are meant to be a united mission, the Church also clearly delineates the necessity for parents to be present with and for their children in this mission of raising them in the faith—in Christ.

- *Catechetical programs are intended not to supplant the role of parents as the primary educators of their children but rather to support and enhance it.* ***In fact, parental involvement in all parish catechetical programs for children is essential.*** (*NDC* #61:4)

- *Even at an age when young children are not yet ready to receive Communion, the Church teaches,* ***"Children who participate with their family in the Mass experience the Eucharistic mystery in an initial way and gradually learn to join with the liturgical assembly in prayer."*** (*NDC* #36:3a)

- *Parish life itself is an aid to parents because it is here, at the Eucharistic banquet, that they are nourished by Christ himself. The vibrancy of the parish community, the beauty of worship and the example of generous love and service of parishioners strengthens parents in the faith.* (*NDC* #54C)

- *Lifelong catechesis should take many forms and use a variety of means; participation in the Sunday Eucharist and study of the Liturgy.* (*NDC* #35D)

- *In the Liturgy, the Church at once expresses her faith and by God's grace deepens that faith. In the Eucharist, Christ leads the community of the baptized to continual conversion in him, to deeper communion with the Father, and to life in the Holy Spirit. The Liturgy both enables and inspires the faithful to live the Christian faith; dedication to the teaching of the apostles, the communal life, the breaking of the bread, and prayer.* ***The participation in the liturgical life of the Church presupposes support of and engagement in all forms of catechetical life in the parish and in the home.*** (*NDC* #39)[21]

Parents can be reminded that through their baptismal promises, they have a duty to bring their children to Mass on Sundays.

- *Baptismal Promise: In asking for Baptism for your children, you are undertaking the responsibility of raising them in the faith, so that, keeping God's commandments, they may love the Lord and their neighbor as Christ has taught us. Do you understand this responsibility?*[22]

C HISTORICAL CONTEXT OF RELIGIOUS EDUCATION AND THE MASS

Support for placing Mass at the center of faith formation programs is also made evident by reviewing the historical development and context of religious education.

Until the 13th Century, On Sundays and Holy Days (Festivals), parish priests were commanded to give religious instruction to the faithful, a natural time to teach as it was a day set aside, by the Lord's own command, to be kept holy and a day the faithful would be at Mass. The Apostles Creed and the Our Father formed the initial general basis of religious instruction, which eventually expanded to include the Commandments, sacraments, the virtues and vices.[23]

In 1562, the Confraternity of Christian Doctrine, CCD (a term still sometimes used today), was established in Rome for the purpose of giving religious instruction which spread over time.[24]

- **Saint Pope Pius X, in 1905 in his Encyclical *"Acerbo Nimis*—On Teaching Christian Doctrine"** instructed that every parish in the world should offer Sunday religious instructions. *"On every Sunday and holy day, with no exception, throughout the year, all parish priests, and in general all those having the care of souls, shall instruct the boys and girls...* ***The instruction must be in addition to the usual homily on the Gospel which is delivered at the Mass..."***[25] Families came to Mass and then were given religious instruction.

- In his encyclical on religious education, it is also interesting to note that **Saint Pius X makes no mention of a lack of Mass attendance** when expressing concerns he has for the faithful. The following is an excerpt from Saint Pius X's encyclical reflecting some of the main moral issues of that time, *"They do not consider it a crime to excite and nourish hatred against their neighbor, to enter into most unjust contracts, to do business in dishonest fashions.......Even if they avoid sensual pleasure, they nevertheless entertain evil thoughts without the least scruple....."*[26]

  This stands in contrast to the great and detailed attention focused on the lack of Mass attendance in more modern documents such as the *DC*, *NDC*, and *GDC*.

Presumably, Mass attendance was not yet an issue in 1905. Although one statistic shows that 90% of Irish Catholics in Ireland attended weekly Mass at the end of the 19th century, statistics for that time period are otherwise not readily available.[27] Regular analysis of Mass attendance rates in the United States began after 1958 when the decline became prominent and, as seen in the chart below, has been on a downward trend ever since.

The original roots of CCD/religious education presupposed that families were coming to Mass every Sunday, which is no longer the case as shown in the chart below. The terminology used in Pope Pius X's encyclical was also indicative of the largely educational component. In today's culture, the knowledge-driven religious education programs have greatly developed over the years but with a reversal in concerns over religious instruction with the sacramental life. Religious education proceeds now without the very heart and essence of Catholicism, the Mass and the full person of Jesus Christ as Eucharist.

FAMILY MASS ATTENDANCE 1958-2021

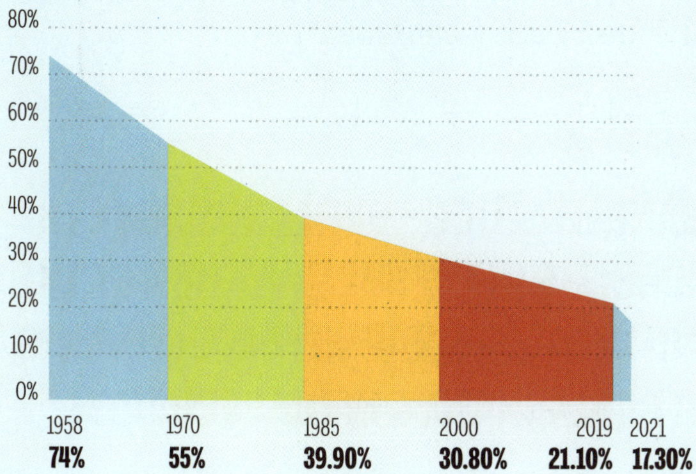

D CATECHESIS AND PRIESTS

As indicated above, historically priests bore the primary responsibility for catechizing the people of God. In *Acerbo Nimis*, Pope Pius X elaborates this point:

- *"There can be no doubt, Venerable Brethren, that this most important duty rests upon all who are pastors of souls. On them, by command of Christ rest the obligations of knowing and of feeding the flocks committed to their care; and to feed implies, first of all, to teach. "I will give you pastors according to my own heart," God promised through Jeremias, "and they shall feed you with knowledge and doctrine." Hence the Apostle Paul said: "Christ did not send me to baptize but to preach the gospel." Thereby indicating that the first duty of all those who are trusted in any way with the government of the Church is to instruct the faithful in the things of God."* (#7 *Acerbo Nimis*)[28]

Over the years, there has been a needed and increased reliance on the lay faithful to provide catechesis. While this is a tremendous blessing, the Church also continues to stress the important role priests have as "educators of the faith."

- *"The function proper to the presbyterate in the catechumenal task arises from the Sacrament of Holy Orders which they have received. Through that Sacrament, priests, by the anointing of the Holy Spirit, are signed by a special character and so are configured to Christ the priest, in such a way that they are able to act in the person of Christ the head'. In virtue of this ontological configuration to Christ, the ministry of the priest is a service which forms the Christian community and co-ordinates and strengthens other charisms and services.* ***In catechesis, the Sacrament of Holy Orders constitutes priests as 'educators of the faith'. They work, therefore, to see that the faithful are properly formed to reach true Christian maturity."*** (*GDC* #224)[29]

A Mass-centered faith formation program opens up opportunities for the parish priest to become a central figure and chief catechist to families, especially through the homily. However, priests, as ordained ministers dedicated to a life of studying the faith, should be welcomed to take on a more prominent role in teaching outside of the Mass.

Father Richard Carton, while pastor at St. Vincent de Paul Parish where this Mass-centered family faith program has been established, advised the following: "Chief among the responsibilities of the priest is to preach and teach. It is imperative that a priest be involved in the faith formation of children and of adults in the parish setting. Through family faith formation centered in the Mass the priest is afforded the precious opportunity to present the beauty and truth of the Christian faith. Then as teacher, he is given the additional opportunity of witnessing in faith to parents and their children. This is an opportunity not to be missed and a responsibility which must be taken seriously. Not only is it a gift to those in formation it also enriches his own priesthood as the spiritual father of those entrusted to his care."

E EVANGELIZATION AND THE MASS

Catechetical leaders strive to combine leading families in the faith with kindness and compassion. The Church describes the very initial stage of evangelization called "pre-evangelization" as one which is ***"built upon basic human needs, such as security, love, or acceptance, and shows how those basic human needs include a desire for God and his word"*** (*NDC*#17C).[30] Suffice it to say "security love or acceptance" are important at every stage of evangelization and natural to what is desired in most human relationships.

"The New Evangelization" a term first used by Pope Paul VI in 1975, has become a central focus in the Church's efforts to bring about "faith and conversion to Christ" in our present culture. (*NDC* #17A).[31] Anyone who works for the Church of recent has no doubt become familiar with this concept and its emphasis on being welcoming and charitable.

While welcoming people at church always will and should remain important, the new evangelization and its various phases must be looked at in a fuller context lest we remain merely hospitable without engaging them more deeply on their journey with Christ.

"FOR IN ITS TOTALITY, EVANGELIZATION—OVER AND ABOVE THE PREACHING OF A MESSAGE—CONSISTS IN THE IMPLANTATION OF THE CHURCH WHICH DOES NOT EXIST WITHOUT THE DRIVING FORCE WHICH IS THE SACRAMENTAL LIFE CULMINATING IN THE EUCHARIST."[32]

Pope Paul VI's Apostolic Exhortation *Evangelii-Nuntiandi* —Evangelization in the Modern World

THE PROCESS OF EVANGELIZATION *(NDC #17C)*[33]

In the various phases of Catholic evangelization, as described in the *NDC*, the path to becoming Catholic involves participation in the Liturgy (Mass) and sacramental life. *"All Liturgy has a catechetical dimension."* (*NDC* #17C)[34]

1. **Pre-evangelization:** First, listeners are prepared for the first proclamation of the Gospel. Pre-evangelization ordinarily builds on basic human needs, such as security, love or acceptance, and shows how those basic human needs include a desire for God and his word.
2. **Initial Announcement:** Then comes the **initial announcement of the Gospel** or missionary preaching. This form of the ministry of the word is directed toward non-believers. **In our age it may also be addressed to those who may have been baptized but have little or no awareness of their Baptism** and who consequently live on the margins of Christian life.
3. **Initiatory Catechesis** follows for catechumens, those who are coming to the Catholic faith from another Christian tradition, **Catholics who need to complete their initiations, children and the young.** The function of the initiatory catechesis is to introduce the life of faith, **the Liturgy** and the charity of the People of God to those being initiated.
4. **Mystagogical or post-baptismal catechesis** is the form of the ministry of the word in which the implications for living a sacramental life are drawn out. The function of mystagogical catechesis is to lead the **baptized deeper into the Christian life, celebration of the sacraments, prayer life of the Church** and her missionary activity.[35]

Children preparing for the sacraments are in the "initiatory" stage of catechesis and certainly should be participating in the Liturgy. But, where do their parents, many or most of whom have received all of the Sacraments of Christian Initiation of Baptism, Eucharist, and Confirmation but often do not come to Mass on a regular basis, fall in these stages of evangelization?

Religious education parents are truly in a unique position in the evangelization process. The Church acknowledges this dimension of evangelization in the United States which *"occurs within diverse and rapidly changing social, religious, and cultural context..."* (*NDC* #17D).[36]

> *The boundaries between and among the diverse social, religious, and cultural context are not clearly definable. In addition, the initial announcement of the Gospel and a basic catechesis, the new evangelization and an initiatory catechesis, and a more permanent catechesis are stages not entirely distinct from one another as dimensions of the Church's mission of evangelization. Catechesis in the United States receives from evangelization a missionary dynamic that encourages us to continue to evangelize the culture, affirming what is compatible and challenging what is* ***not.*** (*NDC* #17D)[37]

What must be considered is the certain level of belief religious education parents already possess in their desire for their children to be formed as Catholics. This simple act of signing up their children for religious education signifies an inner conviction that religion is an important part of their life. This stands in contrast to a highly secularized culture in which an increasing number of parents do not consider religion important in raising children. There has been a dramatic decline in religious education enrollment (statistics, p. 80). Religious education parents, for their children's sake, are very willing to bring them to religious education classes and events although are hesitant in bringing them to Mass. When the Mass is presented as a component of the religious education program, parents will attend Mass with their children. There is an untapped willingness for parents, who sign their children up for faith formation, to be led more deeply into their faith. Parishes must consider this in their efforts to evangelize the whole family.

The *NDC* goes on to state:

> *All dioceses and parishes, in the efforts and resources they focus on the new evangelization, should pursue the following fundamental objectives: (#4) To rededicate themselves to a liturgical renewal that develops a greater appreciation for the presence and power of Christ in the word of God and the sacrament of the Church, especially the Eucharist,* ***and a stronger commitment to celebrating the Eucharist each Sunday.*** (*NDC* #17E)[38]

The program described herein exemplifies the notion that families absolutely can and should be taken further along than we are presently taking them in the process of evangelization. The Church clearly defines the fact that the Liturgy, the Mass, is and has historically been an essential component of catechesis as well as the pertinent phase(s) of evangelization that families are in.

F OCIA—THE CHURCH'S "MODEL OF ALL CATECHESIS"

The process of evangelization as articulated by the *DC* and *NDC* is echoed in the Order *of Christian Initiation of Adults*. Catechetical leaders should take particular interest in reviewing the OCIA because:

- ***The Church recommends that the "model of all catechesis" is the catechumenate. According to ancient tradition, every form of catechesis should be inspired by the catechumenate model.*** (International Council for Catechesis)[39]

- *The RCIA, by the Congregation for Divine Worship on 6 January 1972, has proved especially useful for catechetical renewal.* (GDC#3)[40]

The Catechumenate is the process by which the Catholic Church brings unbaptized adults and children of catechetical age to Christian Initiation[41] *"The term catechumen is to be strictly reserved for the unbaptized who have entered the catechumenate and who are joined to the Church in a special way while they strive to lead a life of faith, hope, and charity"* (*OCIA*, Norm 3).[42]

As seen in the *Order of Christian Initiation of Adults*, one of the primary means of catechizing and forming the catechumenate in the Catholic faith is their exposure to and participation in the Sunday Liturgy:

- *. . . catechumens, whom Mother Church already embraces as her own with her love and care, and who are joined to her, already belong to the house of Christ, for they are fed by the Church with the word of God and the aid of the liturgy.* (OCIA #47)

- *Among the rites belonging to the Period of the Catechumenate, Celebrations of the Word of God are foremost.* (OCIA #79)[43]

Catholic parishioners most likely, at some point, have witnessed adults in their community take part in the OCIA process. Typically, catechumens, after having participated in the Liturgy of the Word at Sunday Mass, are then dismissed for a catechesis. Naturally, faith formation families, who are already Catholic, should participate in the entire Mass, including the Liturgy of the Word and the Liturgy of the Eucharist. It is interesting to observe, however, the contradiction between catechumens (becoming Catholic), whose primary means of formation is through immersion in the Sunday Liturgy versus the faith formation families (already Catholic) whose primary means of formation is the classroom model with Mass participation largely in absentia (statistics, Chapter 3).

Thomas Morris, author of *The RCIA: Transforming the Church* offers interesting insights into the that connect to religious education programs. Morris served as Executive Director of the North American Forum on the Catechumenate. This organization fostered the full implementation of the *Rite of Christian Initiation of Adults* in thousands of parishes in the United States and Canada from 1983–2013.[44] In his book, Morris addresses concerns over the standard classroom model in religious education sacramental programs. "By placing such formation in a strongly "academic" setting, we risk losing the vital link with the primacy of the liturgical celebrations."[45]

KEEPING THE LORD'S DAY HOLY—OUR ENCOUNTER WITH THE LIVING GOD

> ***"To keep holy the Lord's Day, from the very beginning of the Period of the Catechumenate certain provisions should be made."*** (OCIA #83)[46]

"Begin with the End in Mind." Thomas Morris explains a wise principle in "leadership and management" is to begin with the end in mind. *"In effect, the recommendation is to look at the outcome of any project to decide the best way to cause that outcome."*[47]

Dr. Steven R. Covey, author of *The 7 Habits of Highly Effective People*, further supports this concept. He states, *"People are working harder than ever, but because they lack clarity and vision, they aren't getting very far. They, in essence, are pushing a rope with all of their might."*[48]

So let us begin with the Last Supper, the first Mass in which Jesus gave us His body, blood, soul and divinity as Eucharist. Jesus said, "This is my body, which will be given for you; do this in memory of me"(Luke 22:19). **Jesus' life on earth culminated in leaving us Himself in and through the Mass. The celebration of His Eucharistic Sacrifice on the Lord's Day is essential to our identity and mission as Catholics.**

> ***Liturgy is the summit toward which the activity of the Church is directed; at the same time it is the font from which all her power flows."***
> (*Sacrosanctum Concilium*, #10)[49]

Through the Liturgy, we are formed and equipped to be disciples of Christ.

> ***Charity, justice and evangelization are thus the normal consequences of the liturgical celebration...*** (*STL* #9)[50]

WE BECOME WHAT WE DO.

In *RCIA Transforming the Church*, Morris states:

- *"In and through the celebration of the Christian sacraments, we encounter, and are encountered by the living God so we might be the same for the world. Sacraments have less to do with what we get and more to do with who we become in relationship to the holy."*[51]

- *"How we pray (action, symbol and words) forms people more deeply than all those lectures and classes. How we pray forms people's deepest structures of beliefs."*[52]

In an address to parents, when this program began to make Mass a priority, I explained how the actions we participate in at Mass awaken in us, both children and adults alike, to the reality that God is in our midst. "When we come together to worship and give this time to God at Mass, we are truly acknowledging His presence. We all face the altar, we bow, we bless ourselves, and we kneel because of this actual presence before us—our almighty and loving God."

THE LITURGICAL YEAR:

Father Ronald Lewinski (1946-2017), was a well-respected expert in the Church on the catechumenate.[53] In his book, *An Introduction to the RCIA: The Vision of Christian Initiation*, he states, **"One of the *most effective means of catechesis during this period is to follow the rhythm of the liturgical year....*** *Keeping the Lord's Day holy and observing the feasts and the remembrance of the saints unfolds the profound mystery of Christ day by day."*[54]

Morris (*RCIA, Transforming the Church*), further elucidates the importance of the liturgical calendar:

> **Echoing the insights of the Constitution on the Sacred Liturgy, n102, the General Norms for the Liturgical year and the Calendar states:**[55]

- By means of the yearly cycle, church celebrates the whole mystery of Christ, from his incarnation until the day of Pentecost and the expectation of his coming again. (*GNLYC*, n.17)

- Concerning Ordinary Time, it states that "apart from those seasons having their own distinctive character, 33 or 34 weeks remain in the yearly cycle that do not celebrate a specific aspect of the mystery of Christ. Rather, especially on the Sundays, they are devoted to the mystery of Christ in all its aspects. (*GNLYC*, n43)[56]

It is with no wonder the Church wants all catechetical programs to be inspired by the catechumenate model. **Only through the Mass** can a person be fully formed as a Catholic. It is here that one ultimately learns from, is formed by, and becomes one with the Master Catechist, our Lord, Jesus Christ.

As the whole mystery of Jesus is revealed through the liturgical calendar, there can also be a consideration to include participation at Mass on all Holy Days throughout the year. This can happen beyond the weeks when classes are in session and is in keeping with following Christ's commandment and the teaching of the Church:

- *On Sundays and other holy days of obligation the faithful are bound to participate in the Mass.* (CCC #2180)

- *The Sunday Eucharist is the foundation and confirmation of all Christian practice. For this reason the faithful are obliged to participate in the Eucharist on days of obligation, unless excused for a serious reason (for example, illness, the care of infants) or dispensed by their own pastor. Those who deliberately fail in this obligation commit a grave sin. Sunday is a time for reflection, silence, cultivation of the mind, and meditation which furthers the growth of the Christian interior life.* (CCC #2186)[57]

With the clear knowledge and understanding that the ***"object of catechesis is communion with Jesus Christ"*** (*NDC* # 19)[58] catechetical leaders can be confident in following the Lord's command and the Church's directives in developing Mass-based faith formation programs: "*I am the light of the world. Whoever follows me will never walk in darkness, but will have the light of life*" (John 8:12).

G CONFIRMATION AND THE MASS

Confirmation often marks the end of a student's participation in his/her parish's religious education program.

The *Catechism of the Catholic Church* states: "*.... catechesis for Confirmation should strive to awaken a sense of belonging to the Church of Jesus Christ, the universal Church as well as the parish community. The latter bears special responsibility for the preparation of confirmands*" (*CCC* #1309).[60a]

At the Confirmation Mass, the Catechetical leader affirms to the Bishop the following: "*Your Excellency, I am pleased to present to you the candidates for the Sacrament of Confirmation from ______ Parish. I testify that they* ***have been suitably prepared*** *to receive the gifts of the Holy Spirit in the Sacrament of Confirmation.*"

In accordance with all that the Church teaches and instructs in its catechetical mission, Catechetical leaders, in testifying to the Bishop that their students are suitably prepared and formed as Catholics, have a loving responsibility to know their Confirmation students are coming to Mass.

> **"The Challenge to our communities is to remain faithful to the rhythm of the liturgical calendar even and especially when it stands in contrast to the standard calendar with its feasts and images; The Easter Bunny, Santa Claus, summer vacation, the school year and the like."**
>
> (Morris)[59]

- According to the ***Code of Canon Law*** **889-2:** *To receive Confirmation lawfully, a person who has the use of reason must be suitably instructed,* ***properly disposed*** *and able to renew the baptismal promises.*[60b]

- **"Properly Disposed"**—Inherent in this language is that students are in union with Church teaching and are keeping the Lord's Day holy.

- *"Father Charles Grondin, an apologist for Catholic Answers, states, "it is the duty of the parish priests to be sure that the child is properly disposed to receive the sacrament of Confirmation (canon 843 §2). A pastor could legitimately question the proper disposition of someone asking for Confirmation who fails to regularly attend Mass, explicitly denies the faith, expresses desire not to be confirmed, displays an exaggerated ignorance of the faith, or other similar actions."*[61]

In order to give legitimate witness to the Bishop on behalf of students, it is well within reason to ascertain that they participate at Mass via a sign-in system or simply by knowing and seeing them at Mass.

H LEADERSHIP IN AND THROUGH CHRIST

The Church's own voice explicitly instructs that Mass is essential in catechesis and evangelization, and historically this has been the case. Yet too often there is no serious requirement in faith formation programs for families to come to Mass when they are knowingly rarely attending. There is a natural human desire to avoid controversy. However, being in a position of authority, such as an executive, business owner, teacher, or coach, sometimes calls one to the uncomfortable task of

confronting those who are not meeting expectations. Although difficult, where would any business, team or student be if not challenged to be better or to rise to the occasion.

While someone may recognize truth in a situation, avoiding an issue for the sake of getting along is not an uncommon human response. Perhaps, in an effort to build relationships first, parishes avoid pursuing a more direct approach to having families come to Mass because of an unfounded fear that families may walk away forever with no other chance to evangelize them. However, this approach has led to the very result parishes had hoped to avoid. In the past two generations, there has been a dramatic decline in weekly Mass attendance. **There have been devastating moral consequences to a culture that has largely turned away from Christ's presence at Mass.**

Catechetical leaders can be further inspired by contemplating the magnificent graces, both here on earth and for all eternity, a Mass-centered program can open up for souls by reflecting on Jesus' words to Saint Faustina:

- *"I want to tell you that eternal life must begin already here on earth through Holy Communion. Each Holy Communion makes you more capable of communing with God throughout eternity."*
  (Saint Faustina Diary, #1811)

- Jesus told Saint Faustina that He wants to *"lavish My graces upon them (in Holy Communion)."* [62] As catechetical leaders, let us at least give Jesus this chance to.

The program detailed herein demonstrates that when **Mass is the central required component in faith formation, evangelical and catechetical opportunities open up for the entire family. God's grace becomes the sure foundation in opening hearts to building relationships with Christ and the faith community**. In reading this book, it is with all hope that catechetical leaders will feel encouraged, strengthened, and compelled to make the Mass the primary component in faith formation programs.

Throughout the history of the Church, many conversions to the Catholic faith are inspired by witnessing the strong faith of others. Church Father, Tertullian said *"The Blood of the martyrs is the seed of the Church."* [63] The Greek translation of the word *martyr* is to be a witness. **When we, as catechetical leaders stand firmly on the importance of Mass and make it a requirement of our faith formation programs, we are witnessing to families just how essential the Mass is to their salvation in Christ.**

- *In its initial stage, the new evangelization responds to a demand that the Church* ***have the courage to rise to the occasion in order to take bold steps in revitalizing her spiritual and missionary vocation.*** *Christian communities, affected by the strong social and cultural changes taking place, need once again to find the energy and means to ground themselves solidly in the presence of the Risen Christ, who animates them from within. They must allow themselves to be guided by his Spirit so that they can newly experience the gift of communion with the Father which is theirs in Jesus Christ, and, in turn, offer to others this same experience as the most* ***precious gift that can be possessed.*** (The New Evangelization for the Transmission of the Christian Faith #46) [64a]

When we truly believe this, every part of our being should long to center our religious education programs on Jesus through the Mass. This book is a call for Catholic parishes to restructure their programs on the source and summit of all life in Christ—the Holy Mass.

Do we believe that we cannot live without the Eucharist just as we cannot live without water? **Saint Pio said, "The earth can survive more easily without the sun than it can without the Holy Sacrifice of the Mass."** [64b]

As detailed in this book, challenges may come in switching to a Mass-centered program. However, there is no doubt the more dependent I have become upon Jesus, the greater the good he has brought to every situation. I have increasingly immersed myself as often as possible in Eucharistic Adoration and daily Mass praying for faith formation families and the for holy wisdom and courage to do what is needed. I encourage other catechetical leaders to have great hope by holding fast to their prayer life and trusting deeply in Jesus. With God's grace comes a conviction and a passionate abiding charity in courageously leading others to their salvation in Christ. What a joy it is to see families coming Mass!

3 The Catholic Challenge AND A PROMISIMG SOLUTION

ALARMING STATISTICS

- **17% Weekly Mass Attendance among Catholics.**[65]
- **31% of Catholics believe in the Real Presence of Christ in the Eucharist.**[66]
- **60% Catholics never participate in Confession or do so less than once per year.**[67]
- **80% of cradle Catholics no longer consider themselves Catholic by age 23.**[68]

In 1958, 74% of Catholics attended Mass each week.[69] In the past, the standard classroom model of education may have worked because parents took their children to Mass regularly on Sundays. The present-day 17% weekly Mass attendance rate indicates that the majority of Catholics do not understand nor believe in the necessity of living a sacramental life for the salvation of their souls. Astonishingly, only about one-third of Catholics actually believe in the Real Presence of Christ in the Eucharist!

A 2018 article in the *National Catholic Reporter* cites studies showing a near 20% of U.S. teenagers and young adults (ages 15-25 years old) are former Catholics and the median age many stopped identifying as Catholic was 13 years old![70] While the overall cultural trends have a great influence in shaping minds of all ages, a decision made at such a young age most certainly can be attributed to the attitude and practice of the faith by their parents.

In truth, today's students of the faith are rarely living the faith. It should not be surprising that so many young adults abandon coming to Mass and eventually their Catholic faith all together so soon after receiving the Sacrament of Confirmation.

> **"Some secularized societies have lost the sense of Sunday illuminated by the Eucharist. This is a shame! In these contexts it is necessary to revive this awareness, to recover the meaning of the celebration, the meaning of the joy, of the parish community, of solidarity, of the rest which restores body and soul. Of all these values, the Eucharist is our guide, Sunday after Sunday"** (Pope Francis, General Audience, December 13, 2017).

A Promising Solution

In response to the present-day challenge of a diminished faith among Catholics, the Catholic parish faith formation (a.k.a. religious education) program described in this book is a promising solution to renewing the Catholic faith life among families. Termed "Family Faith," this innovative approach to religious education moves beyond a sole reliance on the classroom model for children and teens and *brings the entire family, parents and their children, into both learning and sacramentally living the Catholic faith, inclusive of attending Mass.*

"Catechesis for adults, since it deals with persons who are capable of an adherence that is fully responsible, must be considered the chief form of catechesis. All other forms, which are indeed always necessary, are in some way oriented to it..." (*GDC*, #59)[71a]

THE GRADUATION MENTALITY

In an effort to research new, more effective approaches to religious education, Father Richard Carton, while pastor at Our Lady of Mount Carmel Parish in Boonton, NJ, sent me (as Director of Religious Education or DRE at the same parish) to a national convention on "Lifelong Faith Formation" in 2011.

Parents are dedicated to the religious education process as they believe this is for the benefit of their children.

There was a great eagerness and openness among those present to learn of new approaches in religious education in hopes of ultimately leading families to more fervently practice their faith by coming to Mass. As mentioned in the introduction, DRE's from across the country all collectively shared similar concerns and frustrations about religious education.

These same concerns were expressed at a 2016 Catechetical leaders' meeting in the Diocese of Paterson. During a discussion on the problem of so few religious education families attending Mass, one DRE exclaimed, "I feel like I am drowning!"

It is completely understandable that catechetical leaders, both locally and nationally, express this common frustration in seeing their holy efforts bearing limited fruit.

Further, DRE's from across the nation reflected on the "graduation mentality" regarding the Sacrament of Confirmation.

Statistics have confirmed these somber observations. Parents want their children to learn about God "to be a good person" but do not necessarily associate being a kind and godly person with the sacraments or coming to Mass. A recent study conducted across multiple faiths (referred to on next page) found that religion for nearly all parents was mostly about being a good person, not a personal encounter with God or Jesus.[71b] In reality, however, the deepest charity towards one's neighbor starts with having Christ in one's heart and soul.

The Good News

There is good news in all of this... Parents are dedicated to the religious education process as they believe this is for the benefit of their children. **Therefore, it is through the religious education program that parents, both the nominal and dedicated Catholics, can be reached out to and drawn into a fuller experience of their Catholic faith.** Evangelization of this group of Catholics is key in re-inspiring an important segment of the Catholic population as to the beautiful truths of their Catholic faith.

"Parents are the primary educators of their children... The Christian community must give very special attention to parents. By means of personal contact, meetings, courses and also adult catechesis directed toward parents, the Christian community must help them assume their responsibility."
(*GDC* #226, 227)[72a]

NATIONWIDE: A SHIFT IN CATECHESIS

A national faith survey, including multiple faiths, was recently conducted and analyzed in the 2021 book, *Handing Down the Faith—How Parents Pass Their Religion on to the Next Generation*.[72b] The study revealed the following three key determining factors, consistent in all major faith traditions, in handing down the faith, from one generation to the next whereby children will continue to practice and live the faith into adulthood:

1. Families talking daily about religion in the home.
2. Parents attending religious services at least once a week (Mass for Catholics).
3. Religious faith is extremely important to parents.

The Church has consistently taught that parents *"are the primary educators of their children...and that the childhood religious awakening which takes place in the family is irreplaceable."* (GDC #226)[72c]

Catechesis in, with, and of the Family

In the new Church's *Directory for Catechesis*, directives are presented for catechesis in the family, *with* the family and of the family. (#227-231)[72d]

- *Believing parents, with their daily example of life, have the most effective capacity to transmit the beauty of the Christian faith to their children. "Enabling families to take up their role as active agents of the family apostolate calls for an effort at evangelization and catechesis inside the family."* ***The greatest challenge in this situation is for couples, mothers and fathers, active participants in catechesis, to overcome the mentality of delegation that is so common, according to which the faith is set aside for specialists in religious education.*** *This mentality is, at times, fostered by communities that struggle to organize family centered catechesis which starts from the families themselves. The Church is called to cooperate with parents through suitable pastoral initiatives, assisting them in the fulfillment of their educational mission to become above all the first catechists of their own children.* (*DC* #124)[72e]

There has been a nationwide shift in catechesis towards incorporating parents and their children into faith formation programs. The goal of Family Faith is twofold:

1. Find creative ways to invite parents into the structure of religious education to instill in them the importance of the parental role as the primary influence of their child's faith life. After all, no voice is more influential in a child's life than that of a parent because **no person in the world has been designated by God to love his or her child more deeply.**
2. To educate and inspire parents in the truths of the Catholic faith in an effort to ultimately bring them back to the fullness of Christ's love through participation in the sacraments, especially weekly Sunday Mass and the regular reception of the Sacrament of Reconciliation.

The *Directory for Catechesis* speaks of family faith. *"Intergenerational catechesis envisions the journey of faith as a formative experience not aimed at a particular age group but shared among different generations within a family or a community, on the pathway marked out by the liturgical year"* (*DC* #232)[72f]

Standard Family Faith Model

The Center for Ministry Development promoted a model that replaces the classroom model and asks faith formation families to come together approximately once a month from September to May for a two-and-a-half-hour interactive education session for the whole family inclusive of a meal. This has caught on in parishes throughout the country. Lisa Anslinger, a speaker at the national Catholic family faith conference that I attended and author of *Here Comes Everybody*, which described her experience with whole community catechesis in the parish, said her parish experienced an increase in Mass attendance over time. However, she said there has been no statistical data collected in the country on the impact of this particular faith formation model.

Only Part of the Solution

On the other hand, in speaking with local New Jersey parishes that have incorporated this model for many years, DRE's have explained that their families are coming to the Family Faith sessions but in large measure still not coming to Mass. I actually visited parishes to observe this model in action. On one Sunday morning, after observing a two-and-a-half-hour session, I got in my car to leave and just as I started to turn on the ignition, I stopped because of what I was witnessing. I could not believe the large number of families who immediately got into their cars and left the parking lot instead of going as directed to the Mass that followed. I decided to wait and see just how many walked into church. A total of twenty out of about 200 people from the Family Faith session went to Mass.

Even at the parish where I worked, St. Vincent de Paul, initially most families chose to go to the Family Faith sessions and skip Mass. It was not until the Family Faith sessions were centered around the Mass, and Mass became a requirement, that many more families attended Mass.

"I AM THE WAY, THE TRUTH, AND THE LIFE."

The goal and entire point of educating parents is and should be to bring them back into the fullness of living the spiritual pillars of the faith. While this is an important step in the right direction because parents are also being educated in the faith, it is only part of the solution.

A MORE DIRECT PLAN

In the present culture, it appears necessary to lead families more directly to the following six spiritual pillars of the Catholic faith:

- **Sunday Mass**
- **Reconciliation/Confession**
- **Rosary**
- **Eucharistic Adoration**
- **Stations of the Cross**
- **Divine Mercy Sunday**

This new model that Father Richard and I began in its infancy at Our Lady of Mount Carmel (in 2010) but fully developed at St. Vincent de Paul Parish (since 2013) addresses this head on by laying out a comprehensive faith formation plan to incorporate living these pillars of the faith as a family.

Faith formation classes, which remain as part of this multi-faceted program, take place on Sunday mornings centered directly on the Mass.

Diocese of Paterson Promotes Family Faith

The Office of Catechesis for the Diocese of Paterson, in efforts to promote Family Faith, recommended that diocesan religious education programs incorporate a combination of both Family Faith sessions and age-level classes.

In order to encourage parishes to start implementing this model, I along with my co-worker at the time, Cheryl Wallace, (from 2010-2013), were asked to present the theory of and our experience with Family Faith to DRE's and pastors in the Diocese. These presentations were given at St. Paul Inside the Walls Evangelization Center in Madison, NJ, on three occasions over a three-year period.

However, after having implemented Family Faith at Our Lady of Mount Carmel in Boonton, Father Richard moved to St. Vincent de Paul Parish in Stirling and asked that I join him there. In starting this process all over again in 2013, very important and more promising developments were made over a four-year period that continue to this day. The theory of and methodology is described in this book.

THE PRIEST—A VITAL COMPONENT

A vital component in effectively implementing this program is the parish priest. He will become a central figure and chief catechist through families' participation in the spiritual pillars, most especially Mass, as well as his presence at Family Faith sessions.

The following pages present a detailed look at this new program and the necessary steps, controversies, and resolutions that helped create a new and unique program where Mass, and therefore the full presence of Christ himself is now truly at the center.

4 Family Faith FORMATION COMPONENTS

Faith Formation Components:

1 Catholic Spiritual Pillars
2 Learning & Fellowship Family Faith
3 Age Level Classes

1 SPIRITUAL PILLARS St. Vincent de Paul's faith formation program includes participation, as a family, in the following six spiritual pillars of the faith:

- **Sunday Mass:** Families attend weekly Mass during the entire program.
- **The Rosary:** Families pray a decade before each Mass and the entire Rosary in October.
- **Eucharistic Adoration:** Families come to adore Christ in the Eucharist each year.
- **Reconciliation/Confession:** Families scheduled to come once per year during Lent.
- **Stations of the Cross:** Families scheduled to attend one Stations during Lent.
- **Divine Mercy Sunday:** Families participate in Divine Mercy parish prayers.

Some Catholic parishes schedule students to come to Stations of the Cross or Reconciliation/Confession as part of faith formation. However, this new approach places that responsibility on parents by scheduling them, through the faith formation curriculum, to participate with their children in these events.

2 FAMILY FAITH SESSIONS Parents are asked to accompany their child(ren) with other families in the parish to enjoy lunch and fellowship while engaging in an all-ages faith learning experience. Families are asked to participate in approximately two, two-hour sessions each year depending upon their children's ages.

- **Advent Session:** 1st-5th grade families (topic varies each year).
- **Lent Session:** 1st-10th grade families (topic varies each year).
- **Theology of the Body (Intro):** 6th-7th Family Session (session repeats)
- **Theology of the Body (Advanced):** 8th-10th Family Session (session repeats)

3 AGE LEVEL CLASSES Children attend fewer age-level classes and for a shorter class period than is typically experienced in most religious education programs. This is because Family Faith sessions take the place of classes. Classes and the Family Faith sessions are importantly centered directly around each of the Sunday Masses.

A Faith Formation Schedule is on the next page reflecting how these three components are incorporated.

SAMPLE FAITH FORMATION SCHEDULE

In a traditional religious education program, students are dropped off by their parents to approximately twenty-five or more weekly classes during the year. Parents are also, in large measure, not bringing their children to Mass on Sundays. In conclusion, there is limited or no involvement on the part of the majority of parents. What is amazing to consider is that at St. Vincent de Paul Parish, parents are essentially involved in every aspect of this program. Each session, whether it is a class or a Family Faith event, involves the presence of a parent, and Mass is an integral part of these sessions. **Parents spent from 30 to 37 hours at church during the faith formation year between coming to Mass, engaging in the spiritual pillars of the faith and learning about Catholicism with their children at Family Faith events.**

The following structure allows families with children of all ages to worship and learn together as a family. There are three Sunday session choices:

1st-10th Grade Faith Formation Schedule: Sunday Mass included in time frame

1st-8th Grades 8:15-10:00 a.m. Session Inclusive of 8:30 a.m. Mass	1st-8th Grades 10:15-12:00 Noon Session Inclusive of 10:30 a.m.Mass	1st-10th Grades 5:45-7:30 p.m. Session Inclusive of 6:00 p.m. Mass

Arrival, Mass lesson, Rosary decade: Families arrive 15 minutes before the Mass of their chosen session starts. For attendance, they check off their family name in the church gathering space and then sit in the pew as a family. At this time, there is a brief teaching on Mass which is followed by the parish community praying one decade of the Rosary. This concludes five minutes before Mass starts.

Mass: 8:30 a.m., 10:30 a.m., 6:00 p.m.

Class session: Immediately after Mass concludes, students go directly to their classroom for a thirty-minute classroom session (9:30-10:00 a.m., 11:30-12 noon, 7:00-7:30 p.m.)

Parents: Because the class time is short, many parents choose to stay to enjoy coffee, pastries and fellowship in the school library. They are also given an opportunity to watch a 15-20-minute video on the Catholic faith.

Oct. 1	**MASS, WELCOME & ROSARY** - All Grades & Parents 10:15-12 noon OR 5:45-7:30 p.m. in church
10/8	Mass only (4-day weekend in schools)
10/15	Mass/Class
Tuesday, 10/17	**Family Faith** 9th & 10th Grades & Parents: Respect Life Speaker (7:00-8:30 p.m.)
10/22	Mass/Class
10/29	Mass/Class
11/5	Mass/Class
11/12	Mass/Class
Tuesday, 11/14	**Family Faith** - 6th & 7th Grades & Parents: Theology of the Body (6:45-8:30 p.m.)
11/19	Mass/Class
Saturday, 12/2 or Sunday, 12/3	**Family Faith** - 1st-5th Grades & Parents: "Our Blessed Mother, Fatima and the Rosary" Choose one: Saturday 5 p.m.-7:45 p.m. or Sunday 10:30 a.m.-1:30 p.m. (Mass & Dinner/Lunch included)
Sunday 12/10	Optional Event: 1st-5th Grade Christmas Pageant
12/17-12/31	Mass only - Christmas Break
1/7/2018	**Family Faith** MASS & EUCHARISTIC ADORATION - All Grades & Parents 10:15-12 noon OR 5:45-7:30 p.m. in church
1/14	Mass/Class
1/21	Mass/Class
1/28	Mass/Class
2/4	Mass/Class
2/11	Mass/Class
2/14	ASH WEDNESDAY Mass or Service
Lent:	**Family Faith Reconciliation/**CONFESSIONS - 2ND-10TH Families - Any Monday or Saturday in Lent
Fridays in Lent	**Family Faith** STATIONS OF THE CROSS - All Grades & Parents - Come to at least one Friday Stations.
2/18	Mass only: President's Weekend
2/25	Mass/Class
Mar 4	Mass/Class
Sat, 3/10 , Sun, 3/11 or Sun 3/18	**Family Faith** - All Grades & Parents: "The Miracle of Confession and the Effects on our Souls" Choose one (four choices): Saturday 5-8 p.m.; Sun 3/11 10:30-1:30 p.m.; Sun 3/18 10:30-1:30 p.m.; Sun 3/18 6-8:50 p.m. (Mass & Dinner/Lunch included)
3/25 & 4/1	Palm Sunday - Easter
4/8	**Mass and Family Faith** DIVINE MERCY SUNDAY - All Grades & Parents 3-3:30 p.m. in church

5 Spiritual Pillars

"RELIGIOUS EDUCATION" VS. "FAITH FORMATION"

While the name "Religious Education" is synonymous with "Faith Formation", using the term "Faith Formation" has a broader meaning that encompasses more than just being educated. Changing the name is important in today's culture to communicate to families that being formed in the faith is also about experiencing and participating in the six core spiritual pillars of the Catholic faith.

1. Mass
2. Rosary
3. Eucharistic Adoration
4. Reconciliation/Confession
5. Stations of the Cross
6. Divine Mercy Sunday

MASS AS THE CENTER OF FAITH FORMATION— "I AM THE WAY THE TRUTH AND THE LIFE"

Pillar 1

This program focuses on reclaiming Sunday as the Lord's Day by offering faith formation classes on Sunday centered around each of the three Sunday Masses. Additionally, and very importantly, Mass attendance is a requirement of the program. While we could not fully anticipate how well parents would respond to this new approach, it has been amazing to see the church packed at each Sunday Mass with families when faith formation is in session.

Well over 90% of families are present in Mass when faith formation is in session. Families check off their names, which are located in the gathering space to the church. A visiting priest, who traveled all over presiding at Masses, was present at one of St. Vincent de Paul's evening Masses and stated he could not believe what he was seeing as there was standing room only. He exuberantly expressed he never saw a Mass, other than at Christmas, so filled with families and to keep up whatever it was we were doing.

We gradually transitioned from weekday classes to a Sunday-only program over a four to five-year period. Chapter 8, "The Transition," provides a detailed look and analysis of the transition and the reasoning behind our firm resolution and ultimate success in placing Mass at the center of the program.

ROSARY—MARY LEADS US TO JESUS

Pillar 2

One decade of the Rosary is prayed before each Mass during the faith formation year. A different mystery is introduced each week. Children and/or families are invited to lead the Rosary decade.

Since 2013, St. Vincent de Paul parish begins the faith formation year in October with families praying the Rosary together as a faith community. A brief lesson on the Rosary or Mary is taught to everyone followed by the recitation of the Rosary. Prior to St. Vincent de Paul Parish, this session was first introduced at Our Lady of Mount Carmel Parish in Boonton in 2010.

Bishop Serratelli, in support of Family Faith, attended a Rosary family Faith session at OLMC in 2012. He gave a talk on the Rosary and then led all families in the Joyful Mysteries while kneeling before the Tabernacle. It was inspirational to all. The picture below is taken from the Diocesan newspaper article written on this topic (*The Beacon* 12/20/2012).

Bishop Serratelli leading Our Lady of Mount Carmel families in the Joyful Mysteries of the Rosary.

Parishes should begin with the Rosary Session before introducing a major, two-hour Family Faith session

At the diocesan presentations I gave on this new model of family faith formation, parishes were encouraged to begin introducing the concept of Family Faith with the Rosary prayer session because of its simplicity and importance. This session is a link between the "spiritual pillar" component and the "learning" component. This session serves two purposes:

1 Praying (and learning) the Rosary lays down a foundation of grace by opening up hearts and minds to a willingness and desire to learn more about the Catholic faith.

Saint Pope John Paul II wrote, in his apostolic letter, *Rosarium Virginis Mariae, "The Rosary of the Virgin Mary, which gradually took form in the second millennium under the guidance of the Spirit of God, is a prayer loved by countless Saints and encouraged by the Magisterium. Simple yet profound, it still remains, at the dawn of this third millennium, a prayer of great significance, destined to bring forth a harvest of holiness."* [73a]

As God's very own mother, Mary is full of grace, Queen of Heaven and earth, and greater in holiness than all the angels and saints. Of all of God's creatures, she is the one, our greatest intercessor, who can lead us most perfectly to her Son, Jesus.

In Saint Louis de Montfort's book, *The Secret of the Rosary,* he recounts our Lady's message to Saint Dominic in the thirteenth century, who was discouraged because people were not listening to the Gospel message he was preaching. The Queen of Heaven told him that before people will listen to truth and act in truth, they must first be blessed with divine grace from Heaven. *"My Son," said the Queen of Heaven, "prayer and penance are the only way to win souls. Pray my Psalter (Hail Mary) and teach it to your people. This prayer will never fail."* 73b,c

"....praying the Rosary together as a family is very beautiful and a source of great strength."—Pope Francis, Mass for the Family Day, October 27, 2013

Religious Education student choosing a Rosary at the Family Faith session directed by the Bishop.

In addition, one of the greatest witnessed miracles from Heaven to earth was the Miracle of the Sun at Fatima in 1917. **The Blessed Mother said this miracle happened so that the world would believe her messages. She stressed that people must pray the Rosary every day.**

As a family prayer, Saint Pope John Paul II's wrote, ***"As a prayer for peace, the Rosary is also, and always has been, a prayer of and for the family. At one time this prayer was particularly dear to Christian families, and it certainly brought them closer together. It is important not to lose this precious inheritance. We need to return to the practice of family prayer and prayer for families, continuing to use the Rosary."*** (Rosarium Virginis Mariae)[74]

Families should be encouraged to pray the Rosary at home. If they are new to this prayer, tell them they can start with a decade of the Rosary and build from there. The Rosary is an invitation and opportunity for families to come together and lovingly unite their voices in prayer to Heaven as they reflect on the life of Jesus. There is a beautiful sense of peace that comes from praying this prayer as a family and an intrinsic understanding, for both parents and children, that the family's concerns, hopes and dreams have been placed above our own human limitations and into the supernatural heart of our dearly Beloved Mother and her Son, Jesus.

2 Introduces the concept of Family Faith in a very simplistic manner. Faith formation families are brought together for approximately 30–45 minutes to briefly learn about the Rosary and then pray the Rosary in union with their children and the wider parish community. Logistically this is simple for a DRE to plan. It will also serve to instill a confident understanding that families will and do respond to such an invitation when it is part of the faith formation curriculum.

"I HAVE A BURNING THIRST TO BE HONORED BY ALL IN THE BLESSED SACRAMENT."

Christ to Saint Margaret Mary Alcoque

EUCHARISTIC ADORATION

Pillar 3

Faith formation families, after returning from Christmas break, begin the New Year with a session on Eucharistic Adoration. Immediately after the morning and evening Masses, Father Richard provides a catechesis on Eucharistic Adoration and leads everyone in adoring Jesus through prayer, song and meditation. Families are taught to place themselves in the complete presence of Jesus and simply share with Him what is on their hearts and minds. They are given moments to quietly embrace the comfort and love of Jesus. This session, is *approximately* one-half hour in length.

The Eucharistic Adoration session was first introduced (as part of faith formation) in the 2015–16 formation year. A few parents were brought to tears explaining they had never prayed to Jesus in this way. Immediately after the session was over, one mother expressed, "I have never experienced this (adoring Christ in the Eucharist). When Father lifted up the host (the monstrance), I was brought to tears. This was so beautiful."

In a letter from the Vatican, Pope John Paul II emphasize the importance of being drawn closer to Jesus through Eucharistic Adoration:

> **"I urge priests, religious and lay people to continue and redouble their efforts to teach the younger generations the meaning and value of Eucharistic adoration and devotion. How will young people be able to know the Lord if they are not introduced to the mystery of his presence?**

> **"[...] By learning the words of the prayer of the heart, they will be closer to the Lord, who will accompany them in their spiritual and human growth. ... All interior life needs silence and intimacy with Christ in order to develop.**

> **"This gradual familiarity with the Lord will enable certain young people to be involved ... and to take a more active part in Mass; for young boys, to be near the altar is also a privileged opportunity to hear Christ's call to follow him more radically in the priestly ministry.""**[75a]

SAINT POPE JOHN PAUL II

> **"...let us rediscover Eucharistic Adoration, which continues the work of the Mass within us."**

POPE FRANCIS, CORPUS CHRIST HOMILY, JUNE 14, 2020

THE SACRAMENT OF RECONCILATION/ CONFESSION

Pillar 4

Considering that 75% of Catholics come to Confession less than once per year or never, this Sacrament needs to be addressed and encouraged.[75b] Confession as a "Family Faith" experience is an extremely important and effective way to evangelize families on the importance of this Sacrament. In the Diocese of Paterson, Confessions are held in each parish every Monday evening during Lent. Incorporating this into the schedule was handled differently at the two parishes I worked at but brought many families back to the sacrament who had not been there in years.

Our Lady of Mount Carmel Parish, Boonton, NJ (Lent 2013)

As part of the new faith formation schedule at OLMC, families were assigned alphabetically to attend one Monday night Confession during Lent. This was to help manage the number of people anticipated to come each week. The following sheets were available:

- **Examination of Conscience sheets for various age levels.**
- **"How to Go to Confession" sheets with the Act of Contrition**

In prior years, one priest was able to handle the number of people who came to Confession on Monday evenings. However, during Lent of 2013 when this was introduced it was necessary to have three priests available to hear confessions each week.

I was not sure if attendance sheets should be put out, but it was interesting that so many parents, as they entered the doors, asked where they could sign in so their child could get credit for being there. Some may reason that confessions may not be valid because parents and children were required to come as part of the program. However, once a person enters the confessional, it is up to the priest to discuss and discern if the person is open to the forgiveness of Christ through this sacrament. If not, at the very least, this can be an opportunity for the priest to educate the person more about this sacrament as well as to pray for his/her future willingness to confess.

While there were those who choose not to come, for the families that were willing to participate, parents, both here and at St. Vincent's, expressed appreciation for being led back to Confession. **The general reason parents gave for avoiding Confession for years was an uncomfortableness or slight fear in stating one's sins. One parent said she only came because she is a dutiful parent who follows what is on the schedule for her child's sake. However, after she went,**

FAITH FORMATION PROGRAM

Many of these parents never would have come to receive the Sacrament of Reconciliation if they were not led there through the faith formation program. Approximately 50–60% of families came that first year it was introduced on the schedule. **One of the visiting priests could not believe what he was seeing and wondered how it was possible that so many parents and children were coming to Confession. He saw people who had not been to Confession in ten or twenty years. He said these were good, valid Confessions.**

In Lent of 2018 and 2019, the number of priests rose to six and it still took three hours to hear confessions!

she said she felt wonderful and was so very grateful for being brought to this opportunity. She felt that she was now over her fear of the Confessional.

St. Vincent de Paul Parish (Lent 2015-2019)

At St. Vincent de Paul Parish, attendance is not taken for Confession. Families come on any Monday or Saturday that is convenient for them. Although there is no accounting for how many people are actually coming, it appears an increasing amount of families are participating in this sacrament since it was placed on the faith formation schedule in 2015. This is evidenced by the fact that the priests who are hearing confessions, have to stay longer each year. The Tuesday before Easter, additional priests are available because many families like to come at this time. In 2017, four priests heard Confessions for close to three hours each in one evening.

The increase in participation is not only because it has been on the faith formation schedule, but especially as a result of the importance Father Richard places on the Sacrament through his powerful words on this subject at Mass each year. Priests, through their homilies, can reach many people by speaking about this largely ignored sacrament. Since families are also now coming to Mass, they actually hear Father's homilies and have a chance to be influenced by his words and God's grace.

STATIONS OF THE CROSS

Pillar 5

Faith formation families are required to attend the Stations of the Cross on one Friday evening during Lent. This takes place from 7:30-8:00 in the church. They are also invited to attend the 7:00 p.m. Friday evening Mass during Lent.

For attendance, parents simply check off their name in the church vestibule. Someone from the religious education program is there to greet them. A few parents of young students shared that they had not gone to Stations of the Cross since they were children. Many parents have expressed that they and their children are spiritually moved when they reflect on the Stations.

As of 2018-19, we added Stations of the Cross for children (who came with their parents) on one Friday from 4:30-5 p.m. This earlier option was well attended and appreciated.

DIVINE MERCY SUNDAY

Pillar 6

For the past few years, St. Vincent's Faith Formation Program has concluded on Divine Mercy Sunday. Families are required to come from 3:00 to 3:30 p.m. to participate in the veneration of the Divine Mercy Image and a sung Chaplet followed by Benediction. They are also invited to come to the Exposition of the Blessed Sacrament which begins at 2:00 p.m.

Saint Pope John Paul II instituted this important feast day in the year 2000. Jesus told Saint Faustina, "The Feast of Mercy emerged from My very depths of tenderness. It is My desire that it be solemnly celebrated on the First Sunday after Easter. Mankind will not have peace until it turns to the Fount of my mercy."[76]

THE PRIEST—A MORE CENTRAL FIGURE

What is beautiful about these six spiritual Family Faith events is that the parish priest, an integral part of each session, has the opportunity to more prominently lead faith formation families to a deeper experience and understanding of their faith.

6 Family Faith Sessions

NATIONAL MODEL & DIOCESAN RECOMMENDATIONS

In addition to the spiritual Family Faith events described in the previous chapter, St. Vincent de Paul additionally asks families to participate in approximately two, two-hour Family Faith sessions each year.

The Center for Ministry Development created a model of Family Faith, whereby parents of children enrolled in the parish's religious education program are asked to come together with other families as they share a meal together and participate in learning about and sharing their Catholic faith. The recommended length of these sessions is two to two-and-a-half hours each. Below is CMD's recommended time frame.

While The Center for Ministry Development's model recommended parishes replace classes with these Family Faith sessions occurring monthly from September through May, DRE's were also highly encouraged to find variations of this model depending upon the needs and means of each parish.

Diocese of Paterson

As mentioned previously in this book, I was asked by the Diocese of Paterson to promote the successful program I started between 2010-2013 that combined Family Faith sessions with grade level classes. That combination has worked very well. It is also appropriate to alternate between Family Faith sessions and weekly classes so that both are not running concurrently.

FAMILY FAITH SESSIONS

Part 1	Meal/Community Building Prayer	40 minutes
Part 2	All-ages learning experience	20 minutes
Part 3	In-depth learning experience	60 minutes
Part 4	Sharing learning experience and home application	20 minutes
Part 5	Closing Prayer	5-10 minutes

PRIEST INVOLVEMENT

At the Center for Ministry Development's lifelong faith formation conference, the absolute importance of the parish priest's presence at Family Faith events was stressed. It does not have to be for the entire session (although this is welcomed). However, if possible, it is recommended that the priest give a blessing to the families present and speak, even if briefly, on the faith topic for the session. Parents are more likely to embrace this approach when the priest shows his support and is present.

FAMILY FAITH TOPICS

Session topics should be varied and rotate in a cycle of approximately 6-10 years (depending upon grade levels involved), so that a family will only attend the same session once. Curriculum for sessions should be based on themes from the *Catechism of the Catholic Church*:

- The Profession of Faith
- Liturgy & Sacraments
- Morality
- Christian Prayer

There is no shortage of Catholic faith topics. The challenge is in coming up with sessions that inspire and teach families authentic truths of the Catholic faith. Everyone must feel engaged from the first grader to the adult.

Having two themes per school year allows the director of religious education to spend the necessary time researching each topic as well as thinking through how to engage each age level. Catechists can provide excellent insights and ideas for crafts and methods of teaching. However, the subject matter taught must reflect Catholic doctrine and the DRE must be involved in creating or at least approving what will be taught.

Father Richard speaking at a Family Faith Session.

SERVICE PROJECTS AND FAMILY FAITH SESSIONS

Family Faith sessions can also include opportunities for service projects. Although most parish Confirmation programs incorporate works of charity, all grade levels and entire families can be encouraged to participate. Ideas can be inspired from and support the charity driven ministries of the parish. For example, during Advent, we asked families to participate in the "Giving Tree" project by donating Christmas gifts for the poor. Students were also asked to make Christmas cards for the homebound of our parish. One of the religious sisters on staff, who directs the food pantry and social outreach, personally delivered the cards. She spoke to the families at a family faith session and explained how these spiritual bouquet Christmas cards were met with delight and even tears of joy from those who received them. She gave families a presentation on religious life and the many Works of Mercy they are involved in.

PROCEED CAREFULLY

> **An important lesson given by the many parishes in the country that have already embraced some aspect of Family Faith.... PROCEED CAREFULLY when implementing Family Faith.**

One of the reasons catechetical leaders were all strongly encouraged and even warned to move slowly when introducing Family Faith was because of the experience some of those on the forefront of this new concept had when they first introduced it to their parish. Parishes who transitioned too quickly (within a year), from a traditional weekly class program to a once a month family faith program, essentially took families by surprise and many walked away. Parents were upset because their presence was expected at these sessions. However, it was interesting to hear how these same parishes witnessed many of their families coming back over time. Those who experienced Family Faith were starting to enjoy it and the word spread. Today, some parishes have a waiting list to get into their Family Faith program.

Respect the intelligence of your parents by informing and educating them as to the theory behind and method that will be applied at Family Faith sessions. This can and should happen via parent meetings at the beginning of the religious education school year. Start slowly, perhaps with one major Family Faith session at some point during the school year. Work as a staff to ensure this first session is one that families feel their Catholic faith has been deeply enriched by. Once families begin to understand and appreciate a Family Faith session, add additional sessions the following year. During the weeks when Family Faith sessions take place, the age-level classes should take a hiatus.

These sessions are an amazing opportunity to evangelize Catholics. It is important the material presented reflects what it fully means to be Catholic.

FAMILY FAITH IMPLEMENTATION AND PARISH MODEL

Open Invitation

Our Lady of Mount Carmel Parish in Boonton, NJ had its first two-hour Family Faith session in April of 2011. (It should be noted this followed the first and simpler "Rosary" Family Faith in December of 2010). **It was marketed as an open invitation** to families to participate in a fun and faith-filled family event. Notices were placed in the bulletin and flyers were sent home to religious education families. It was **NOT** a part of the religious education program at that point. Sixty-five people total (adults/children combined) signed up and came. This relatively small number was great for the staff of four (including the priest) who were excited and nervous, as it was the first time running such an event.

Expected Participation

Having gained confidence from running one, for the following religious education year, OLMC incorporated two Family Faith sessions into the Religious Education program, one occurring during Advent and one during Lent. **Because these sessions were part of the religious education schedule, parents knew they were expected to participate.** As previously mentioned, a presentation was made to parents at the beginning of the religious education school year as to the theory behind Family Faith. Parents were asked to participate in this new approach and told their feedback would be important in determining the effectiveness of Family Faith. During Advent three sessions in one weekend were offered to accommodate all the families that were to attend.

OLMC hosted another Family Faith session during Lent. Once again, three sessions were offered in one weekend. Families were assigned alphabetically to a session. However, if they were unable to attend the assigned session, they were allowed to choose another.

Attendance

Approximately 65-70% of families participated in the very first session and the feedback was very positive. Within a short time of two years, these sessions became more popular and well attended. Due to the increase in those interested in attending, the number of sessions rose to six over a period of two weekends to accommodate the number of people in attendance.

Two-Hour Family Faith Session Sign-ups at OLMC:

The below sign-up percentages do not represent the attendance rate. While most people attended who signed up, there are always last-minute absences due to illness and other family urgent matters. It's good to keep in mind that the typical absentee rate for daily public school attendance is approximately 8%.[77] The main point to glean from this information is that families increasingly signed up for Family Faith as a reflection of the positive experience they had at these sessions.

After June of 2013, I left OLMC and started working as Director of Faith Formation at St. Vincent de Paul Parish. We started the year with the Family Rosary session in October. In Lent of

TWO HOUR FAMILY FAITH SESSION

Year	% Families Signed up	# of Sessions	Theme
2011 Advent	70%	3 sessions needed	Jesse Tree
2012 Lent	85%	4 sessions needed	Prayer
2012 Advent	95%	6 sessions needed	Holy Mass
2013 Lent	98%	6 sessions needed	Eucharist

2014, a two-hour Family Faith session was introduced. Eighty-five percent of families signed up exceeding expectations. This is attributed in part to insights gained from executing this program at the previous parish.

Sign-ups through On-line Registration

Since 2017, parents are required to sign up for Family Faith sessions through the on-line registration process on our parish website, so sign-ups are 100%! This has been a much simpler and effective sign-up method.

St. Vincent de Paul Sessions

Since 2013, **the two-hour Family Faith sessions** have evolved into the following sessions. Each family will attend approximately two each year depending upon the grade levels of their children.

Family Grades	Family Faith Description
1st-5th Grade Families	**Advent Session:** Topic changes each year
1st-10th Grade Families	**Lent Session:** Topic changes each year
6th-7th Grade Families Repeats every other year	**Theology of the Body Introduction: *** "Made in God's Image"—This session seeks to lay a very important foundation for sixth & seventh graders of Catholic values that will help students recognize the sacred dignity of themselves and others. The following ideas will be addressed: "Who am I? (my gifts, both spiritual and physical; God has a plan for me; Intellect and Free will; My body, as male or female, expresses my soul; How do I use my body (my gifts) to glorify God and to love and respect others." Modesty in dress will also be touched upon as well as the importance of avoiding movies, television shows, video games, and music that are degrading to the human person. This session will also open up an important dialogue on Catholic morality between a parent and their 6th/7th grade child. Parents will have a wonderful opportunity to affirm their child in the positive values and God given gifts he/she is developing.
8th-10th Grade Repeats	**Theology of the Body Advanced:*** 8th -10th graders and their parents will attend a session that present a deeper level of Theology of the Body. In light of Saint Pope John Paul II's writings, the "whys" behind the Church's beautiful teachings on chastity and the importance of "waiting" until marriage will be explained and discussed as a family and community.

*Catechesis on **Theology of the Body** is a "Priority for the Office of Catechesis." According to the Diocese of Paterson's Catechetical Handbook, "Theology of the Body is a right understanding of our very identity as persons created in the image and likeness of God our creator because we will seldom arrive at our destination if we fail to know where we are from. Theology of the Body helps people to grasp their theological anthropology and to rightly appropriate this understanding into actions for our goodness, happiness and heavenly orientation."

While the majority of parents increasingly appreciated Family Faith, many chose to come to these sessions instead of the Mass. To try to stop this from happening, during the 2016-17 school year we decided to structure the Family Faith sessions (as many as possible) around the Mass by asking families to come ten minutes before Mass starts to pray a decade of the Rosary as they had become accustomed to each week. As a result, many families came directly from Mass to the Family Faith session instead of from the parking lot.

This required a slight adjustment in the time length of the Family Faith session. While they were there from 10:20 a.m.-1:30 p.m., because of the transition from coming over after the Mass ends, there needed to be flexibility with the amount of content being taught. If a Mass on a particular Sunday got out later because of a Baptism, it was fairly easy to consolidate some of the teaching content so that families still could leave by the designated end time of 1:30 p.m.

FAMILY FAITH FEEDBACK

Asking parents to come to a two-hour Family Faith session during Advent and one during Lent does not pose any strong time burdens on families. At the beginning some parents admitted they were not sure if these sessions would be worth their while to come to as they felt their lives were just too busy. However, afterwards, many gave wonderful feedback as to how important they felt these sessions were for the following reasons:

- **Parents were inspired by what they learned about the Catholic faith.**
- **They enjoyed discussing the faith with their children.**
- **Many felt it was important and enjoyable discussing the faith topics with other families.**

The following emails were addressed to me in response to asking for feedback on the two-hour Family Faith sessions that religious education families attended in the 1st through 8th grade program (In OLMC the Family Faith was 1st-10th). Assurances were given that emails will remain anonymous.

FAMILY FAITH—GENERAL COMMENT

- **Parent of 6th Grader:** *"I have to tell you I went to CCD until 6th grade that is when I made my Confirmation and I really feel I didn't know anything about my faith until my children started CCD. I know it is*

extremely hard to cram everything in but the fact that you have the children saying the rosary and talking about praying is great! I never did the rosary growing up. It was never taught to me, so I am benefiting from all your sessions just as much or more so then my daughter. I believe the sessions provide a fun way to get them to learn about their faith in a different environment."

THE HOLY MASS (2012 & 2014) FEEDBACK

- **Parent of 1st thru 7th Graders:** *".....As far as the church portion of the presentation I am in awe. In over 40 years of a Catholic upbringing including attending CCD for many years, taking part as a sponsor in an RCIA program and having four children in Catholic School I have never understood Mass the way I do now. It was such an enlightenment to visualize what each section of the Mass is supposed to evoke in your spirit.......All four of my children from my twelve year old down to my six year old had a great time and learned so much."*

- **Parent of 1st thru 5th Graders** *".... The evening left us with a feeling of being connected more to our family, to the Church and most importantly to God. I really like how the program is designed so that families have to interact with one another and also with the other families attending. Even though you may see the same people in Mass each week, the sharing of dinner together and learning about the Catholic faith together connects us that much more. It's evident that a lot of time, effort and thought are put into planning these sessions and I thank you sincerely."*

- **Parent of 7th Grader** *"I thought the Family Faith session on the Holy Mass was amazing. When I was in church this Sunday, it definitely made me more aware of the spiritual beauty that is happening beyond my line of vision. I can only speak for my child, but my child is in the 7th grade and really enjoyed the program. He not only finds them interesting, but loves when my husband and I get to learn along with him, and truthfully, we do to."*

- **Parent of 1st & 3rd Graders** *"I wanted to share with you how much my family and I enjoyed your program yesterday. As a product of 16 years of Roman Catholic education, four of which were with the Jesuits, and as a daily communicant, I was surprised at what I did not know. The effort you put into the event was glaringly apparent and much appreciated. The "nuggets" that one can glean from such a presentation contributed greatly to a deeper understanding of the tenets of one's religion. Rare are the thank you's or conveyance of appreciation; which is why I felt compelled to share what a positive impact your efforts had on us. I wish you all the best and continued success in your endeavors to improve catechetical education."*

- **Parent of Middle Schoolers** *"Thank you for a terrific program this afternoon. We all learned a great deal. It was especially nice to spend a few hours as a family together... With the hectic schedules we keep; it sometimes can be tough to do."*

"THE MIRACLE OF THE EUCHARIST AND THE EFFECTS ON OUR SOULS" (LENT 2013 & 2016)

- **Parent of 1st-5th Graders** *"My family LOVES the Family Faith sessions! Even my adult children come when they are home. I feel we have learned things such as how to receive communion (why are hands are together and directed upwards, and bowing before) and it has reinforced the knowledge and beliefs I already have. I believe as parents we should be our children's primary CCD teachers. The Family Faith sessions reminds me of this. The break-out sessions help open a dialogue and I think it is beneficial for the younger students especially to have a hands-on activity. "*

- **Parent of 1st-5th Graders** *We have enjoyed the Family Faith sessions!!! We are all running in so many different directions and it is nice to sit and enjoy time with our friends at Church. ...... I feel your break-out sessions really reinforce in a fun way what we are learning."*

- **Parent of 5th & 7th Graders** *"Thank you for all the work you did at The Eucharist Family Faith presentation on Sunday. The late food presented Father Richard with the perfect opportunity to share the analogy of how Jesus is so hungry for our love and the importance of feeding our soul as much as our stomachs. To me everything tasted even more delicious after hearing those beautiful words. I asked my son what he liked best about this Family Faith session. He said the best part was "when we turned the candle on and off to show how when we receive the body of Jesus each Sunday our hearts light up inside like a candle." He is keeping the candle beside his bed now and turning it on when he prays at night."*

- **Parent of 1st & 3rd Graders** *"Thanks for the Family Faith session yesterday. You made it much easier for both children and adults to understand the significance of receiving the Eucharist through fun craft activities and educational videos. Thank you!"*

- **Parent of 1st & 2nd Graders** *"I asked my son what he learned from the Family Faith session and he said, "I learned God's love grows in our hearts." I asked my daughter the same question. "I learned about Jesus and the Eucharist and it's important to go to church." Thank you for all your hard work this Sunday. It was a great afternoon with family, focused on our faith. I learned so much that I really did not know at all, so for that I am grateful!"*

It was a great afternoon with family, focused on our faith.

DIVINE MERCY—THE POWER TO TRANSFORM OUR LIVES (BASED ON THE DIARY OF SAINT FAUSTINA) (LENT 2017)

- **From a visiting Director of Religious Education:** *"Thank you immensely for inviting me to your Family Gathering on Divine Mercy. I cannot tell you how much I enjoyed the whole session… Father Richard gave such a vibrant talk with such enthusiasm. He is so genuine and very welcoming. I loved how the families know exactly what to do in a simple and elegant setting! The children too were very friendly and open to come and say hi… I enjoyed speaking with the Confirmation Student Volunteers. They were about serving and seeing that all bases were covered."*

- **Parent of 6th& 8th Graders** *"Thank you, Deirdre. Today was a beautiful day. Thank you for your efforts and the efforts of all those involved in putting today together. We had a great time and it reminded us how much we love being part of the community at St. Vincent de Paul."*

JESSE TREE SESSION (ADVENT 2011)

- **Parent of a 6th Grader** *"What a great event!!! I felt a real sense of togetherness, especially with the children/parent participation. It was so nice to be involved in a session with my daughter and my husband. She even commented on how it was nice to have us there."*

- **Parent of 4th & 6th Grader** *"…On a personal note, I have a challenge having my husband participate in the religion for our family…but he went to Jesse Tree and REALLY enjoyed it. He was also an active participant on Saturday (Prayer FFS). So thank you for helping us to bring our family together like this, if only a couple of times a year."*

PRAYER SESSION (LENT 2012 & 2015)

- **Parent of 6th Grader:** *"…Job well done. Each member of my family walked away with a good feeling inside! My pre-teen daughter wrote the most beautiful and thoughtful prayer. It made my husband and me cry…it should make you feel so good that you were able to connect with audiences of all ages!"*

- **Parent of High Schooler & Middle Schooler:** *"I really enjoyed our time on Saturday. One thing I really liked was the group discussion time…I liked the idea of sharing ideas with other adults, hearing the ideas of children and everyone's thoughts on prayer. To me, it has always been a very personal, intimate practice that I have only talked about with my immediate family. Nice to hear other opinions and practices."*

- **Parent of 6th Grader:** *"I just wanted to thank you again for a wonderful program yesterday. We all enjoyed learning about prayer and meeting a new family in the process."*

- **Parent of 1st-5 Grade Children:** *"The prayer books were a fabulous idea! They are something we will always cherish. We also loved the personal stories—they made the power of prayer so real for the* children, too."

- **Parent of 8th Grader** *"The lasting gift will be the prayer book we made. We worked very carefully together on it. I was touched by the prayers my son chose, and the meaning behind them for him. I will encourage him to always keep it nearby. Last but not least, I will always cherish the prayer my son wrote for me. Such a sweet sentiment, in his own handwriting, it perfectly captured this moment in time when we were so close in our faith. I'll look forward to attending another Family Faith Service in the future."*

ANGEL SESSION (LENT 2016)

- **Terry Leing, Religious Ed, St. Lawrence the Martyr, Chester NJ** *"St. Lawrence used the Angel session this past Advent season and it was a wonderful experience. The families that attended all enjoyed it and many parents were surprised that they too learned new facts about angels. Of course, everyone loved to hear something we were told as children-that we all have a guardian angel. The children always like the craft/activities that are part of the program and the angel bookmarks were no exception.*

  The sessions you have shared with us have become a wonderful teaching moment for the families of our parish. You have made it so easy to implement that it's actually a fun experience for not only the families, but for me too! Families left with not only a new found knowledge of angels but also a sense of comfort knowing that God has sent each of us an angel to watch over us as we move through our life here on earth."

  Thank you so much for all the work you do in putting these family sessions together."

Families left with... a sense of comfort knowing that God has sent each of us an angel to watch over us as we move through our life here on earth."

- **Parent of 7th Grader** *"Thanks for a wonderful program yesterday morning! I enjoy these family programs very much and feel better knowing about my guardian angel—something my grandmother used to always believe in but I had let it slip away from my faith. My daughter enjoyed it too and we really enjoyed being together. Thanks for doing all that you do! I really believe that the past two years with all the faith opportunities I have explored that I have grown in my faith. "*

- **Parent of 2nd Grader "***We enjoyed learning about Angels!! It gave both of us a lot to talk about. Great Event!"*

SAMPLE FAMILY FAITH FORMATION FLYER FROM 2017-2018

This informational flyer provided to families describes the Spiritual and Learning Family Faith components of the program:

St. Vincent de Paul's 1st–10th Grade faith formation offers a unique combination of classroom sessions and Family Faith events. Family Faith, described in detail below, is designed to help foster a deeper understanding, love and sharing of the Catholic faith for the whole family and parish community. This format promotes the family as being the most important influence in a child's faith life.

Part I: Spiritual Family Faith

The following spiritual pillars of the Catholic faith are incorporated and experienced as a family in this program:

Spiritual Pillars	Description
Mass	Mass is at the center of the faith formation. Because of the importance of Mass as the source and summit of our faith and to encourage greater Mass participation, classes are offered in connection with each of the three Sunday Masses.
Rosary	The faith formation year begins in October with the entire community coming together to pray the Rosary. Thereafter, faith formation families will pray one decade of the Rosary just before Mass on Sunday. Our Blessed Mother explained that the great Miracle of the Sun at Fatima happened so that all would believe her messages. She has directed us that the Rosary must be prayed every day. Through the Rosary, hearts and minds will be opened to listen to truth and act in truth so that peace will be obtained in our homes and in the world.
Eucharistic Adoration	In January, families will begin the New Year with a Eucharistic Adoration session. Father Richard will provide a catechesis on Eucharist Adoration and lead us all in adoring Jesus through prayer, song and quiet meditation. This is an important opportunity to contemplate the amazing gift Jesus gives of himself in the Eucharist to each one of us.
Reconciliation/Confession	It is a Church precept to come to Confession at least once a year and anytime one is aware of being in a state of mortal sin. As part of the faith formation program, families are invited to come to Confession during Lent.
Stations	Families are asked to participate in one Lenten Friday evening Stations of the Cross.
Divine Mercy Sunday	Saint Pope John Paul II instituted this important feast day in the year 2000. Jesus told Saint Faustina, *"The Feast of Mercy emerged from My very depths of tenderness. It is My desire that it be solemnly celebrated on the First Sunday after Easter. Mankind will not have peace until it turns to the Fount of my mercy."*

PART II OF FAMILY FAITH FLYER:

Part II: Learning & Fellowship Family Faith Parents are asked to accompany their child(ren) along with other families in the parish community, and enjoy lunch and fellowship while engaging in an all ages faith learning experience. Families are asked to participate in approximately two sessions each year:	
Family Grades	**2017-18 Description**
1st-5th Grade Families	***Advent Session:** "Our Blessed Mother, Fatima and the Rosary"
1st-10th Grade Families	***Lent Session:** "The Miracle of Confession and the Effects on our Souls"
6th-7th Grade Families	***Theology of the Body** "Made in God's Image" —This session seeks to lay a very important foundation for sixth & seventh graders of Catholic values that will help students recognize the sacred dignity of themselves and others. The following ideas will be addressed: "Who am I, my gifts, both spiritual and physical; God has a plan for me. Intellect and Free will; My body, as male or female, expresses my soul; How do I use my body (my gifts) to glorify God and to love and respect others." Modesty in dress will also be touched upon as well as the importance of avoiding movies, television shows, video games, and music that are degrading to the human person. This session will also open up an important dialogue on Catholic morality between a parent and their 6th/7th grade child. Parents will have a wonderful opportunity to affirm their child in the positive values and God given gifts he/she is developing.
9th-10th Grade Families	**Respect Life Presentation** by Guest Speaker

* These sessions written by Deirdre Nemeth. To receive a copy, email her at MassCenteredFF@gmail.com.

7 Age Level Classes

- **While *Pflaum Gospel Weeklies** has been our preferred program, all approved Catholic Religious Education publishers' texts can be used in this program.** An important resource, provided by the USCCB (United States Conference of Catholic Bishops), is the "Conformity Listing of Catechetical Texts and Series" (https://www.usccb.org/resources/CRL) Since the majority of publishers provide enough material for sixty to ninety-minute lessons, the material has to be condensed to fit into a thirty-minute lesson. The catechists are told to review the material and highlight the main points of the chapter in their lessons.

  Classes meet approximately thirteen to sixteen times each faith Formation year due to the incorporation of Family Faith events. In books that provide twenty-five or more lessons, the DRE can choose the essential chapters to be covered.

- **St. Vincent's switched from the spiral approach** since many of the parents and catechists complained that students were becoming bored with the same topics each year.

- **One of the changes made was to introduce the Bible timeline** in 3rd and 6th grades since Catholics should be introduced to the Bible from an early age.

The following is an overview of the curriculum themes for each grade, and which is provided to families in the form of a flyer:

Sample 1st-10th Curriculum Themes
This informational flyer provided to families describes the curriculum themes for each grade: St. Vincent de Paul's Faith Formation combines Family Faith events (described separately) and classroom sessions. Age-level classroom sessions take place immediately after Mass on Sundays beginning in October. While children are in class, parents are welcome to attend an adult faith class or enjoy coffee and fellowship with other parents.

> ***Pflaum Gospel Weeklies**
> The *Pflaum Gospel Weeklies* is a liturgically based catechetical program that helps parents in their important role as the first witnesses of faith for their children.
> **Website:** gospelweeklies.com

Grade	Curriculum Themes
1st	**Our Heavenly Father** Sacramental preparation is a two-year program beginning in 1st grade and concluding in 2nd grade with First Penance and First Eucharist.
2nd	**First Penance and First Eucharist** First Penance is in November First Holy Communion is in May
3rd	**Bible Timeline** An introduction to the Bible and major people and exciting events of the Old Testament leading up to Jesus.
4th	**Themes of the *Catechism*:** 1. God (Father, Son, Holy Spirit) 2. Sacraments & Liturgy 3. Ten Commandments/Morality 4. Prayer
5th	**Consecration to Mary** Mary, as the Mother of God, is the Queen of Heaven and earth and our greatest intercessor. Consecration means to give our hearts and concerns to Mary who will lead each of us to a deeper union with her Son, Jesus.
6th	**Bible Timeline** An overview of the Bible as God's plan to save us from sin and death and bring us to eternal life. The Sacred Scripture is the history of God's Covenant with the Chosen people.
7th	**Themes of the *Catechism*:** 1. God (Father, Son, Holy Spirit) 2. Sacraments & Liturgy 3. Ten Commandments/Morality 4. Prayer
8th	**THEOLOGY OF THE BODY** This curriculum is based on Saint Pope John Paul II's Theology of the Body and sheds a beautiful light on the dignity of each person as being made in the image and likeness of God.
9th/10th	**CONFIRMATION PREP**

8 The Transition

The faith formation program described in this book came to its culmination after a four to five-year transitional period at St. Vincent de Paul Parish. The following is an important look at the transition, including the reasoning for each change, concerns, and controversies and finally a program that makes sense all around. In order to understand the arrival of a thirty-minute class time centered around the Mass as a beautiful solution to "How do we get people to Mass?" it is first helpful to analyze impacts of the 90, 75, 50, and 40-minute class times experienced over a five-year period.

YEAR ONE (2013-14): WEEKDAY CLASSES; MASS ATTENDANCE

During my first year as Director of Faith Formation, Saint Vincent de Paul's schedule was as follows:

1st-5th Grades	1st-5th Grades	6th-8th Grades
Tuesday 4:15-5:30 p.m.	Wednesday 4:15-5:30 p.m.	Sunday 6:00 p.m. Mass Class: 7:00-8:30 p.m.

1st-5th Grade Attentiveness—75-Minute Weekday Classes

On a weekday after school, it is evident that many of the children are tired and prone to being a bit restless especially with the older grades. Some catechists were adept at providing a lesson plan that kept the children active and involved but for others it was more challenging. A few of the catechists took advantage when the weather was nice and taught on the playground for the last fifteen minutes of class when the children found it difficult to pay attention and needed to move around after being in school all day. One year, a few parents whose children simply did not like coming to classes approached me and asked if religious classes could be less like a class and more fun like a club.

Catechists who attended weekly Mass expressed their disappointment that their students were not coming to Mass on any regular basis. One catechist, after teaching for a number of years, resigned at the end of the faith formation year. She explained she just no longer had the enthusiasm to teach students who were not attending Mass and who were not overly interested in the content being taught.

1st-5th Grade Curriculum

The 1st-5th Grade curriculum was a spiral based approach to catechesis (in which the same themes are addressed each year but at a deeper level). Catechists were also taught not to read directly from the books but to incorporate various methodologies in the lesson. The children's behavior, therefore, was not because there was a lack of substantive lessons nor appropriate instructions for the volunteers.

6th-8th Grade Attentiveness - 90-Minute Classes

An hour and a half class on a Sunday evening is too long. While some catechists had a better ability to handle and teach the students for this amount of time, there were behavioral issues. *One Catechist, after attempting to work with and engage the students over many classes, actually walked out and*

1ST-5TH GRADE MASS ATTENDANCE

The weekday Catechists were asked on a few occasions to take informal surveys from the students as to who went to Mass on Sunday. The results were comparable to national surveys. **Approximately 25-30% of students said they went to Mass the past Sunday**. Students who did not come to Mass had no concerns expressing why they do not go to Mass. Reasons given ranged from playing sports, their parents had to go shopping, were visiting relatives or they were just too busy. Catechists had the impression that no one felt any stigma in not attending Mass. After all, this is the cultural norm.

quit during a class because the students continually talked and laughed with each other above the lesson being taught. This catechist acknowledged that the students were good kids but, in this setting, they simply were unmanageable. While this was an extreme case, many catechists have expressed that it is obvious most students were not enthused to be in these lengthy religious education classes. A number of parents complained that this time frame was just too long and their children did not look forward to coming.

6th-8th Grade Mass Attendance

Students were supposed to be coming to the 6:00 p.m. Mass first and then attend the class afterwards. While a number of students did attend Mass, the majority were dropped off at 7:00 p.m. for class. Informal surveys from the catechists on Mass attendance revealed most of the students were not coming to Mass as was seen with the weekday classes (25-30% Sunday Mass attendance).

Additional Observation

It should be noted that many of the catechists are not teachers by profession and even in a public-school setting classes are on average only forty minutes long as compared to the 60-90-minute classes usually experienced in a religious education class.

Considering that most parents were rarely attending Mass, students may also intrinsically feel ambivalent toward the content being taught.

YEAR TWO (2014-15): SUNDAY CLASS; MASS ACTIVITY SHEETS

Changes in bold:

1st-5th Grades	1st-8th Grades	6th-8th Grades
Tuesday 4:15-5:30 p.m.	**Sunday 9:30-10:20 a.m. (8:30 a.m. or 10:30 a.m. Mass)**	Sunday 6:00 p.m. Mass Class: **7:00-8:15 p.m.**

1st-8th Grade Sunday Morning Class—50-Minute Classes

In the hopes of drawing more families to Mass, one of the weekday classes was eliminated and, in its place, a Sunday morning session was added. It was offered for 1st-8th graders and designed to fit in between the two Sunday morning Masses therefore making it only 50 minutes long. Behavior was better and there was an increase in Mass attendance from some of these families. **Unfortunately, a majority of parents made coming to faith formation classes a priority and left after classes were over without attending Mass.** It was not until we added the Mass activity sheets (below) that more families came to Mass.

6th-8th Grade Sunday Evening—75-Minute Classes

We shortened the evening session to 75 minutes, and this was slightly better but still no increase in Mass attendance with this format.

Recruiting Catechists

Sunday: It was easier to recruit catechists for a Sunday morning session because most parents do not work on Sunday mornings.

MASS ACTIVITY SHEETS—TUESDAY & SUNDAY MORNING SESSIONS

To encourage more families to come to Mass, weekly Mass learning activity sheets were distributed to students. These were to be handed back in at the next class. The questions could be answered by attending Mass and they were grade level appropriate. For instance, as part of one Sunday's Mass lesson, fourth through eighth graders were asked to observe the processional and notice where the priest was in the procession and where the cross was placed.

While this did have success in bringing many more people to Mass, a number of parents and students were filling out the sheets at Mass which became distracting. There was also a lot of administrative work involved keeping track of the sheets and some of the older students would write their answers in at the beginning of class by copying from each other.

YEAR THREE (2015-16): A MORE DIRECT APPROACH

Changes in bold:

1st-5th Grades	1st-8th Grades	6th-8th Grades
Tuesday 4:15-5:30 p.m.	Sunday 9:30-10:20 a.m. (8:30 a.m. or 10:30 a.m. Mass)	Sunday **Session: 5:45-7:40 p.m. (Inclusive of 6:00 p.m. Mass)**

6th-8th Grade Sunday Evening Session

Session Structure—40-Minute Classes

As a staff, we decided to take a more direct approach in leading families to Mass. The evening session started 15 minutes before Mass, in church, and class only lasted 40 minutes after Mass. Our goal was to place Mass at the center of faith formation program to encourage greater Mass attendance. Families were required to sign in by checking off their name in the church vestibule.

Essentially, 15 minutes of what used to take place in class, that of reviewing the Mass lesson and praying one decade of the Rosary, would now occur in the church before Mass for the entire family to participate in. We experimented with this change for the middle school Sunday evening session only to see if this theory would work. It was quite successful.

Instructions for Parents

"This session time has been adjusted to include the 6:00 p.m. Mass. Both parents and students are to arrive at 5:45 p.m. to church for a teaching on the Mass and to pray one decade of the Rosary. Class time will therefore conclude earlier this year at 7:40 p.m."

Mass Attendance

At least 90% of students and their parents attended the 6:00 p.m. Mass during faith formation sessions! While not everyone made it to the Mass lesson on time, almost everyone got to Mass (it is not uncommon for students to arrive five minutes late (sometimes more) for weekday classes as well). Evening Mass was often standing room only. As mentioned earlier, during one of these Masses, a visiting priest commented that this reminded him of a Christmas Mass it was so packed with families.

Lesson Plans

Since many of the religious education books provide lessons to accommodate a 60-90-minute class, catechists were told to review the chapter for the main points they needed to cover and make the lesson plan shorter. The catechists had to learn to adjust to this, but they all did and found the classes actually went well and the students were better behaved.

Adult Faith Offered:

During the 40-minute class time, parents were invited to watch a video on Bishop Barron's *Catholicism*. Approximately 10 parents stayed for many of the weeks which was more than we ever had (none stayed for the 50-minute morning session).

BEHAVIOR ISSUES DRAMATICALLY DECLINED ON SUNDAY EVENING

Catechists commented that the students were the most well behaved and engaged they had seen in years. Two catechists, each teaching for over ten years, expressed amazement at how the 8th graders were actually attentive and not prone to fidgeting or playing with their cell phones.

YEAR FOUR (2016-17): ENTIRE PROGRAM AS MASS/CLASS

Changes in bold:

1st-8th Grades	1st-8th Grades	1st-8th Grades
Sunday **8:15-10:00 a.m.** **(Inclusive of 8:30 a.m. Mass)**	**Sunday** **10:15-12:00 p.m.** **(Inclusive of 10:30 a.m. Mass)**	Sunday Session: 5:45-7:40 p.m. (Inclusive of 6:00 p.m. Mass)

All 1st-8th Grade Sessions Centered Around Masses—30- 40-Minute Classes

Since the past year's change to the middle school program went quite well, a decision was made to make the entire 1st through 8th grade program completely centered around Sunday Masses as a requirement (8:30 a.m., 10:30 a.m., 6:00 p.m. Masses). In doing so, Tuesday classes were no longer offered. Parents choose one of the above three Sunday sessions.

FLEXIBLE SCHEDULE

While families had to sign up for one session, they were given the flexibility of attending another session if they had a scheduling conflict on any given Sunday. The idea was to make this flow with the life of a Catholic. While most church-going Catholics attend the same Mass time each week, there are family events that occasionally make choosing a different Mass time more convenient. **The objective was to make sure families did not miss Mass because they could not attend their usual class.** This never posed any problems with the catechists as they were told to be prepared with extra crafts or activity sheets in case another child or two came. Parents also informed us in advance if they were going to switch classes.

Mass Attendance Skyrocketed

This was an excellent move and there was over 95% Mass attendance on most Sundays during the 2016-17 faith formation year of those present! This does not include those families who were absent due to sickness, etc. Also, the majority of families who did not attend Mass, whose first language was Spanish, said they wanted to attend a local Spanish Mass (St. Joseph's Shrine) and then come to the class.

CONTROVERSY & RESOLUTION

Controversial Reaction among Tuesday Parents

While the families already attending a Sunday session were on board and many embraced the new time frame, this move initially caused quite a controversy with the Tuesday families. About twenty Tuesday parents, through a representative, said they intended to leave and attend the weekday religious education program at another local parish because Mass was not involved, and many had sports on Sundays. There was actually quite a discussion on Facebook from those opposed to this change.

Staff's Response & Resolution

As a staff, we discussed this at length as to whether we should move forward but in the end the decision was clear. **We concluded that the standard religious education program for the past forty years has not produced Catholics engaged in the faith and certainly not Catholics who attend Mass regularly.**

If we continue on this path to appease parents with an underperforming program that they have become accustomed to, where are we truly leading everyone?

It was also evident that the weekday model of classes had difficulty in fully engaging students who were tired from being in school all day. Some of the first and second grade students had never even seen the inside of the church until they were given a "Church Tour" as part of the curriculum.

Imagine a sports coach who allowed children to practice only because they and their parents were not interested in participating in the end goal, the game. Well, leaders of the Catholic faith know the stakes are far greater than playing in or winning a sports game. As shepherds of leading souls to their salvation, we need to curtail the long-standing trend of education without engaging in the faith.

St. Vincent's Parish discovered the overwhelming number of parents are indeed willing to be led back to the Mass through the faith formation program.

It is also human nature to complain more than to praise. While it is important to listen and analyze why some may complain, it is also important to realize that far more people may be happy about a situation but will be far less likely to express this than those who are unhappy. There is actually a book titled *Satisfied Customers Tell Three Friends, Angry Customers tell 3000.* [78,79]

Most families appreciated the new 6th–8th grade program that was implemented in the past year. Parents expressed satisfaction because their children did not mind coming to faith classes since they were shorter in length; and we were happy because all families were attending Mass during the program. It seemed to be a win-win.

As mentioned in the introduction, by *placing Mass at the center of the faith formation program, we believed many more souls would be brought directly to the presence of Christ whose grace would work on them in ways that the education portion alone could not*. Additionally, families would have an opportunity to come to know their parish priest as well as be educated by him, as the spiritual leader and chief catechist of the parish, through the homilies. **(Before Mass was a part of the program, there were actually parents and students who did not recognize Father.)** Some families, in the end, may walk away but we thought of all of those students and their parents who would now be led to the fullness of the Catholic faith by both learning about Christ and experiencing Christ.

In the end, only three Tuesday faith formation families left the program because they did not want to come to Mass (there are approximately 270 students in 1st through 8th grades). We even offered them the home-school option and asked that they come to any Mass of their choice (including Saturday). When they declined all options, they were welcomed to come back at any time. However, all the other Tuesday families along with all of the Sunday faith formation families did re-register.

EVERYONE CAME TO MASS

Positive Results—Everyone came to Mass! **For the first time, nearly all of the faith formation families came to Mass when the program was in session!** It was beautiful to see the 8:30 a.m., 10:30 a.m. and 6 p.m. Masses filled with families. During the year, a good number of parents expressed gratitude for this program that brought their family back to Mass.

Anecdotal evidence that consciences are being influenced:

- One mother explained that when she came to Mass after not going for many years, she realized her family belonged here. She was moved by listening to a teaching on the Mass, Father's homily and also felt interiorly moved by the spirit within her during Mass. She went to Confession after Mass and said she has been coming with her family ever since.

- Another parent said from all of St. Vincent's emphasis on the Mass over the past few years, she was starting to "get it" that Mass was important. While her family had not been coming to Mass prior to the program, she said she was now glad to be coming during the program and would try to come more often after that.

- A mother switched to the homeschooling option during the year and explained that coming to Mass would be difficult for her as she worked all week and needed a break on Sundays. However, she and her child did come to the Family Faith sessions (a requirement with the home school option). The following spring, she told me that she had been discussing the faith more with her child at home and through what she learned at the Family Faith sessions this past year (the "Eucharist" and "Divine Mercy") she realized it was good to come to Mass and she has since been taking her child to Mass more often. She now has enrolled her child in the classes and intends to come again on Sundays.

- A Parent smiled and exuberantly said, "I love this program! You are getting all of us to come to Mass!" (Her family did not come after the program but she was just so pleased that they came during the program).

POSITIVE BEHAVIOR & VOLUNTEERS INCREASED

Classroom Behavior was Positive

Students were much more willing to pay attention and participate in this shorter time frame. The behavior issues were greatly reduced. **These students are actually spending more time at church because of coming to Mass for an hour before class but their behavior and interest is at a better level.** It is probably the combination of the grace of the Mass and the fact that the students are changing venues. The fact that the family is coming together to Mass also gives testimony to the children that this is of value to their parents.

Effective Teaching

Some of the catechists are professional teachers and expressed that it certainly was possible to get an effective lesson in this shorter time frame. All the catechists had to learn to adjust the lengthy lesson plans to fit the time frame but everyone said it worked and many said it was actually much better this way.

Volunteers increased!

There was a waiting list of volunteers this past year! While many parishes struggle to get volunteers, we had an abundance of parents willing to volunteer. It was not only that many do not work on Sundays, but parents explained since they will be at Mass anyway and the class time was only 30 minutes, they were willing to stay and help. Volunteer opportunities included, but were not limited to catechists, hallway monitors, coffee/snack set-up and clean-up, and assistance preparing arts and craft projects for Family Faith sessions.

Additionally, because this program is a combination of Family Faith events and classroom sessions, parents are only teaching no more than 13-16 class sessions a year which is much easier to commit to than the standard 25 or more sessions many parishes have. It may seem counter-intuitive, but it is easier to recruit more people than less people with the explanation that there will be two adults in the classroom either as co-catechists or as catechist and aide. Aides are fairly easy to recruit because they do not have the responsibility of planning the lesson. Through their experience of observing and assisting the catechist, when needed, aides are usually willing to substitute for the catechist. Many aides eventually become catechists. Everyone's lives are so busy that knowing there is a back-up plan built into the commitment of teaching is a very attractive component.

BUILDING COMMUNITY & ADULT FAITH

Building Community:

Parents stayed! When the class time is only thirty minutes after Mass, many parents chose to stay and enjoy coffee, pastries and fellowship in the parish library. A total of 45-60 parents stayed each week and another 40+ parents volunteered in the program.

Even for parents who only came to Mass, they were able to witness and experience their entire community worshiping Christ together. What a difference from when many parents only involvement in the parish was to drop off and pick up their child for classes.

Adult Faith Opportunity:

Additionally, a 15–20-minute video was shown on the faith each week and a number of parents actually enjoyed watching the *Divine Mercy* series.

Session	Class time after Mass	# of Parents who stayed after Mass while their children were in class
8:15-10 a.m. *(smallest session)*	30 minutes	~10-15 parents
10:15-12 p.m.	30 minutes	~25-40 parents
5:45-7:40 p.m. *(Largest Session)*	40 minutes	~10 parents*

***After the 6 p.m. Mass:** Only about 10 parents stayed each time and this session had the most students. This is because the session was ten minutes longer than the morning sessions (40 min vs. 30 minutes).

Editor's Note: Each parish and program is different. Thirty-minute class time after Mass works in the Family Faith program examples provided in this book. Adapt according to your needs and what works best for your program.

Contact Deirdre Nemeth at MassCenteredFF@gmail.com or Pflaum Publishing Group at editor@pflaum.com if you need guidance on how to develop a customized lesson plan.

YEAR FIVE & SIX (2017-18 AND 2018-19): 30 - VS. 40 -MINUTE CLASSES

Changes in bold:

1st-8th Grades	1st-8th Grades	1st-10th Grades
Sunday 8:15-10:00 a.m. (includes 8:30 a.m. Mass)	Sunday 10:15-12:00 p.m. (includes 10:30 a.m. Mass)	Sunday **Session: 5:45-7:30 p.m.** (includes 6 p.m. Mass)

- Families arrive to church and sit in a pew 15 minutes before Mass starts. A brief lesson on the Mass is taught, followed by praying one decade of the Rosary. Then Mass begins.
- During the 2017-18 faith formation year, the 9th & 10th Grade Confirmation students who are required to attend the evening session, for the first time, were on the same schedule as the 1st-8th graders. This enabled families with children in all age groups to be able to worship and learn together at the same time.
- The other minor but impactful change that was made was to reduce the forty-minute Sunday evening class to thirty minutes.
- In 2018-19, as permitted by the Diocese of Paterson, St. Vincent de Paul began the transition to 8th Grade Confirmation.

MORE POSITIVE RESULTS!

30- vs. 40-Minute Class Time in Reaching Parents:

For reaching parents to help build community around the Mass and offer them opportunities to learn more about the faith, keeping the class portion to 30 minutes is key. We have experienced 90, 75, 50, and 40-minute classes. While the 40-minute class time encouraged some parents to stay, the 30-minute session encouraged a much larger number of parents to stay (see chart below). In the shorter time frame, many will not have enough time to go home and get something substantial done before having to turn around and come back to pick up their children. In this scenario, it was a joy to see so many choosing instead to enjoy fellowship, coffee, and/or learning more about the Catholic faith.

Session	Year	Class time	Parents who stayed after Mass while their children are in class
5:45-7:40 p.m.	2016-17	**40 minutes**	**10 parents**
5:45-7:30 p.m.	2017-18 & 2018-19	**30 minutes**	**35-50 parents**

ADULT FAITH OPPORTUNITIES

There were so many parents staying and enjoying fellowship during this time, that I postponed introducing a faith-based video. I observed a number of parents introducing themselves to one another during the first few weeks. I did not realize how many knew each other's faces but were unsure of each other's names. The building up of community through fellowship is very important and parents really seem to be enjoying this time to relax and talk.

Below are additional learning opportunities parishes in the Diocese of Paterson offer parents as part of the Mass/class format:

- Parents are given a weekly talk or lesson on the faith from the Priest, Deacon, Director of Faith Formation or a guest speaker.

- Witness talks. Parishioners are invited to give brief witness talks about their Catholic faith to the parents. This is followed up with guided table discussions.

- Ministry speakers: Consider inviting parish or diocesan speakers to introduce and invite parents to become more involved in parish ministries such as the food pantry, art & environment, bereavement, life ministry, Knights of Columbus, etc.

The many ministries of St. Vincent de Paul parish were thrilled to see so many families with children at Mass and saw an opening to make better connections with faith formation families. As a result, I coordinated with our parish ministries to take turns hosting coffee and snacks on some Sunday morning after Mass. By additionally providing information on their charitable organizations, they were successful at recruiting more parents and even students.

Over time, this model builds upon itself in ways that one may not imagine at first. Mass-centered family faith formation opens doors to greater involvement in the wider life of the parish community.

Mass Attendance: Additionally, while reduced class time of forty minutes encouraged many faith formation families to come to Mass (over 90%), the thirty-minute time frame brought the Mass participation a little higher.

INCREASING MASS INVOLVEMENT/ ATTENTIVENESS FOR THE CHILDREN

During the 2018–19 faith formation year, a few parents asked for ways to help increase their children's attentiveness and involvement at the Mass since Mass is a required part of the program.

- **Liturgy of the Word for Children:** Parents volunteered to run the Liturgy of the Word for Children at one of the Masses two Sundays each month. Fourth graders and younger were invited to participate. The feedback from both parents and children of all ages was extremely positive. A fourth grader explained how much he loved having the Bible readings explained to him and that it was great to be able to ask questions.

  We were fortunate at St. Vincent de Paul's to have a small chapel with a Tabernacle attached to the main church where the students can attend the Liturgy for children. We keep the approach very simple and respectful of the sacred place of worship they are in. The readings are proclaimed and the catechist explains their meaning and invites the children to answer and ask questions. Arts and crafts are not involved.

- **Altar Serving Class:** The most involved a student can be at the Mass is as an altar server! To encourage children to serve and learn more about the Mass, on a couple of Sundays, students had the option of attending an altar serving class instead of going to their regular faith formation class. As a result, we recruited a few more altar servers!

  During 2019-20 faith formation year, we took this concept a step further by incorporating altar-serving classes into the curriculum for each eligible grade level. This served to instruct the students about this significant role at Mass as well as encourage them to become altar servers.

  Parishes that institute this Mass-centered model also find it conducive to greater student involvement in other liturgical ministries such as gift-bearers, ushers, greeters, music ministry and lectors.

COVID YEAR—THE DOMESTIC CHURCH AND THE GREATER GOOD

The Domestic Church

Faith formation during the year of the pandemic certainly brought about challenges that led to creative approaches to learning. At St. Vincent de Paul Parish, the home became an even greater center for learning and formation in the faith than in years past. From this experience, I witnessed the positive influence parents have when they become their children's primary catechists.

2020–21: While families remained at home during the pandemic, each family was asked to purchase a Catholic Bible (if they did not already own one and many did not own a Bible). The first Bible assignment was to learn how to navigate the Bible by placing Bible tabs on each book of the Bible. Weekly family Bible lessons were brief (15-20 minutes) which involved answering questions and discussing Bible passages, as a family, related to the Sunday Gospel. Since families were already accustomed to coming to Mass for faith formation prior to Covid, they continued to be connected to Mass by tuning in virtually. Many of the assignments also had questions pertaining the Mass they watched. There were not individual grade level assignments, except for the sacramental preparation years, as I felt this would be overwhelming during the pandemic. It worked quite well as a very large majority of families completed and emailed the assignments to me.

It was a pleasure to read the lessons and get a glimpse into the wonderful family faith discussions taking place. Year-end reflection questions had two common responses: Families shared that they enjoyed participating in the faith lesson together as a family, and many also missed the Church community.

2021–2022: Insights gained from the home learning experience during the pandemic helped influence our approach going forward. The 2021-22 family faith formation year continued to be centered on the Mass as in the past. Families were required to come to Mass every Sunday. However, we did not return to grade level classes that took place immediately after Masses. Instead, to foster the importance of family in being formed in the faith, approximately two Sundays each month, the entire family, after attending Mass, participated in a thirty-minute interactive faith learning session. They brought their Bibles to these sessions. The other two Sundays, home lessons were done as a family during the week and then handed in as they came to Mass.

Can We Watch from Home?

At the beginning of the faith formation year, a small number of families asked if they could continue to watch Mass from home. However, the NJ Bishops reinstated the obligation to come to Mass in June 2021 and I did not have the authority to release anyone from it. So, unless there were serious reasons, everyone was expected to come to Mass and for the most part, did.

There was a brief period in December/January 2022 when many families were quarantining or had contracted Covid due to sharp increase of cases in NJ at that time. However, after Covid slowed down, families did return to Mass. Their attendance was very good considering many had become accustomed to staying at home during the pandemic.

Positive Feedback

Throughout the year, many parents commented positively on their experiences. One father of a 7th grader wrote: *"I think the program you run is beneficial to our younger generation and is taught in a way to include the parents bringing the two together with love in the name of Christ."*

Another father of a 1st grader and a 3rd grader shared that he appreciated that the parent/child conversations they had at the Family Faith sessions came home with them.

Regarding the home lessons, a mother of middle school children said, "I love that the home assignments require and enable us to have good faith discussions at home."

A mother of an elementary age child emailed,

"Thanks for a great year of Family Faith formation. We enjoyed learning and growing as a family this year!"

Fathers—More Present

What I did not anticipate and was pleasantly surprised about was the increase in fathers who came to Mass and the Family Faith sessions compared to prior years when there were fewer Family Faith sessions after Mass. Perhaps this is because a parent's presence was required at the Family Faith sessions compared to the *invitation* to stay while their children were in classes. Over time, I started to see both fathers and mothers together at these sessions since both enjoyed the family interactive lessons and discussions that took place.

This is very good news, especially in light of a study, from Pew Research Center, that concluded, "Most say their parents shared equally in their

religious upbringing, but if one was mainly responsible, it was usually mom."[80a]

Another Pew study revealed that, in Christian populations, women are more likely than men to report attending services weekly.[80b]

Fathers, however, have a particularly strong influence. As reported in the book, *Handing Down the Faith*, "The role of fathers is especially important in forming children religiously. Both parents matter a lot in faith transmission, but the role of fathers appears to be particularly crucial, providing dads (when they are present) with extra influence and responsibility in the matter."[80c]

First Eucharist & Penance Students—Well Prepared

Due to the pandemic, parents took on a greater role in preparing their children for the sacraments of First Reconciliation and First Eucharist. They were responsible for overseeing their 1st and 2nd Grade child(ren)'s reading and activity assignments which were done at home. I had a schedule for them to follow, and their children's completed home assignments were handed in when they came to Mass. At First Reconciliation, the visiting priests expressed their amazement at how well these students knew their Act of Contrition compared to what they experienced at other parishes! This is a result of parents becoming their child's primary catechist. As the new *Directory for Catechesis* states "The greatest challenge in this situation is for couples, mothers and fathers, active participants in catechesis, to overcome the mentality of delegation that is so common, according to which the faith is set aside for specialists in religious education (see statement in full on page 32).[80d]

2022-23: National Eucharistic Revival (Declared by USCCB on Corpus Christi Sunday)

The USCCB has launched a three-year National Eucharistic Revival which began on the feast of Corpus Christi, 2022. We moved forward during the first year of the Eucharistic Revival, keeping in mind the positive impact increased parental involvement brought forth. Saint Vincent de Paul Parish continued to incorporate parents in the thirty-minute sessions after Mass and provided simple yet faith-filled family home assignments. Parents gradually became accustomed to their involvement in the program over the years. These incremental changes have been met with open minds.

9 Mass—A True Starting Point

WHEN FAITH FORMATION SEASON ENDS

After the faith formation season ends, many families stop coming to Mass. While this can appear discouraging, it is important to realize that the trend to not come to Mass gradually declined over a sixty-year period (74% in 1958 to 17% of recent). Reversing this trend will not happen overnight and if it did, that would be nothing short of miraculous. After all, many parents in the faith formation program have parents that did not take them to Mass regularly, so it is somewhat ingrained in people that Mass is a good but unnecessary part of life. Families are also not in the habit of coming to Mass and the fact that families who came a few times a year now come close to twenty times a year reveals that parents are open to being moved in a new direction toward the Mass.

The looming question many parishes have about how religious education families can be brought to Mass can consider this a true starting point.

Creating New Habits:

In *The Happiness Advantage*, Harvard professor and researcher, Shawn Achor, comments on the fact that even though we may be given the knowledge to do the right thing, it is much harder to follow through with the action required.

"As Aristotle put it, to be excellent we cannot simply think or feel excellent, we must act excellently." He goes on to say, "positive habits are hard to keep, no matter how commonsensical they might be... 80% of us break our New Year's resolutions. Even when we feel committed to positive change, sustaining it for any real length of time can seem nearly impossible........Humans are biologically prone to habit and it is because we are "mere bundles of habit" that we are able to automatically perform many of our daily tasks...... It is precisely because habits are so automatic that we rarely stop and think about the enormous role they play in shaping our behavior, and in fact our lives.....Given our natural tendency to act out of habit, couldn't the key to sustaining positive change be to turn each desired action into a habit, so that it would come automatically, without much effort?"

Achor continues, "But how do we create new habits in the first place? A tendency to act only becomes effectively ingrained in us in proportion to the uninterrupted frequency with which the actions actually occur and the brain "grows' to their use." In other words, habits form because our brain actually changes in response to frequent practice." [80e]

Old habits may be hard to break and new ones challenging to establish. However, a program that requires parents to bring their children to Mass each week as part of faith formation allows families to experience the reality and discipline that they actually do have time to get to Mass even though many previously felt their lives were just too busy to come to Mass.

As someone who has been involved in faith formation for over fifteen years at four different parishes, this was amazing to witness and is deeply encouraging. This points to the fact that parents are willing to come to Mass as part of the program for the sake of their children and sheds a hopeful light on the possibility of renewing the faith in a secular culture. The following is an excerpt from one of the Mass lessons I presented to families before Mass began that elaborates on the above idea of developing the habit of worship.

> **"During a recent Mass, I had a sudden and overwhelming appreciation for this gift we have to worship. At a simple level, when we contemplate God's creation from the stars and planets in the universe to the earth and to the intricate beauty of every human, it should inspire within us an awe of wonder of our almighty God. It is here at the Mass that God gives us the ability to express to Him the praise and worship that is due Him. This is a desire that should dwell deep within in our hearts since we were created by God to know Him, to love Him and to serve Him. When we open our hearts and minds to who we truly are in God's eyes, we can come to understand what a sublime joy and gift it is to stand in honor, to bow our heads and to kneel before the True Presence at Mass! Nothing, nothing can compare to Him. Worship reminds us of our total commitment and loyalty to God. Of course, appreciating the gift of showing the reverence to God may happen in steps and gradually grow on us. For instance, before we can appreciate the beauty of playing a wonderful piece of music on the piano or before we enjoy perfecting our athletic skills on the field, we practice over and over again and sometimes it seems difficult. It takes discipline but over time, we develop a wonderful skill. Well, the same can be said for developing an appreciation for the beauty and importance of Worship. So at the Mass, let us pray that God leads us to a deeper appreciation of this gift as we join the angels and saints in Heaven in adoration and worship of our one true God."**

Prayer

It will of course take time, effort and prayer to see Christ's truths and life develop more fully in everyone. As Saint Paul reminds us, "you need someone to teach you the elementary truths of God's word all over again" (Hebrews 5:12).

In reviewing the results of the new structure of the program, the staff concluded that bringing everyone directly to Christ at Mass was good and necessary. At one point, we decided to encourage willing members of the parish to pray for everyone's conversion toward a greater appreciation of the importance of keeping the Lord's Day Holy. On the 2017–18 & 2018-19 registration form, parents were presented with an opportunity to participate in Eucharistic Adoration during the thirty-minute class time as follows:

Eucharistic Adoration Prayer Volunteers:

"A Holy Hour before the most Blessed Sacrament so pleases the Heart of Jesus, that every man, woman and child on earth receives a new effect of God's graces" Saint Faustina.

Will you consider, while your child(ren) are in faith formation classes, to spend a few minutes or a half hour in the Eucharistic Adoration Chapel to pray for your own family as well as for the grace that all parish families come closer to the Eucharistic Heart of Jesus?

During those years, approximately 15-20 parents signed up to pray for this intention!

It should be noted that families who already come to weekly Mass greatly appreciate the opportunity for Eucharistic Adoration. Right from the beginning, they have consistently shown enthusiasm and great support for this Mass-centered program that places the Eucharistic at the heart and center of faith formation.

Going forward, we will be taking this program another step forward by requiring families to attend Mass all year (in other words by checking in during the summer months as well). While there has been a slight increase in the amount of families who continue to come after faith formation has concluded in the spring, there is still a noticeable drop off in Mass attendance after April. Father Richard believes, and I concur that our families who have become accustomed to coming to Mass each week from late Sept/Oct thru April are ready for the requirement of attending Mass all year.

Why Parents Accept or Embrace the Program

Even though some families do not come to Mass on their own accord, many of these same families are accepting and others embracing this program. It is a program designed to bring families back to the spiritual pillars of the Catholic faith but with the understanding that families are also burdened with many time constraints. St. Vincent's program begins close to October 1 with a community Rosary and concludes on or shortly after Divine Mercy Sunday.

Parents appreciate the fact that they can settle into the public school year first before faith formation begins and have also expressed they and their children feel the year concludes at a more reasonable time frame than traditional religious education programs. Even though the length may be shorter in duration, this is still a program in keeping with the Diocesan time guidelines and more importantly, perhaps the only program that parents actually participate in all aspects inclusive of Mass, spiritual pillars and the learning components.

Parents have also said the combination of classes and Family Faith events keep the program more interesting than traditional religious education programs. They are glad to see their children are not complaining about coming anymore. Some said their children enjoy coming with this new format.

Participation in the spiritual pillars is bringing parents directly in touch with our living God. Even souls, not previously interested, must perceive this at some level and are opening up to the effects of God's grace.

10 Mass vs. Standard Religious Education—A Competition?

A typical religious education program in this country actually competes with the Mass because of the large amounts of time children are expected to be in class. *Since many parents do not understand the importance of Mass or the sacraments, they have allowed class to supplant the Mass.* It should not be either or since both aspects are important. Parents worry about their child(ren) accumulating too many absences. Since missing a faith class is not a mortal sin but Mass is, restructuring the program with Mass as the most important part makes so much sense.

While the concept of mortal sin in relation to deliberately missing Sunday Mass is perhaps rarely understood or embraced today, this Mass-centered model provides ample opportunity to teach families why the Mass and the Eucharist are essential to our life in Christ.

Why do we avoid more directly leading families to what we know is the sure path to salvation?

Father Richard Carton, a priest of 31 years and pastor, shares, "As a Mother, the Church teaches that participating at Mass fulfills the Lord's command that we keep holy the Sabbath, and Jesus's instruction that we 'Do This in Remembrance of Him."

"The importance of this is underscored by the reminder that we are obliged to participate and not to participate intentionally deprives us of that full and intimate encounter with Christ, truly present in the Eucharist, which the Fathers of the Second Vatican Council teaches is the source and summit of all life within the Church. We draw our very life from the Eucharist, so how can we be intentionally absent and still draw that life?"

Many catechetical leaders and pastors, locally and nationally, in reflecting upon the fact that most faith formation families do not come to Mass, will shrug their shoulders and repeat an all too accepted mantra "well people can't be forced to come to Mass." Words we choose to use and accept have a very powerful influence on how we think and act. For instance, the word "fetus" has greatly assisted in de-emphasizing the humanity of the unborn child.

A simple definition of the word *forced* on Google reads:

> ***"Obtained or imposed by coercion or physical power. The brutal regime of forced labor."***

The word *forced* is often used to describe a terrible situation a person is being subjected do against their will. The connotations of the word *force* stop many catechetical leaders and pastors in their tracks from more directly leading families to the Mass.

Even though it is mandatory for students to attend a certain number of days at public school each year, would any reasonable parent say, "My child is being forced to go to school." This would be an inaccurate and inappropriate use of language. Children are not always enthusiastic about getting up and going to school every morning but no responsible parent would question the great value and importance of education by using the word "forced" to describe the requirements to attend school.

So why do we in the Church accept language that subliminally suggests people are being brought to experience something violently against their will? Jesus Christ, who is Love itself, is waiting in His fullness at Mass. Paradise opens before us at Mass to a heavenly banquet. Divinely magnificent gifts of graces are showered upon each and every person. The Mass is to faith formation what education is to the public-school system. Why do we avoid more directly leading families to what we know is the sure path to salvation?

Perhaps it is falsely reasoned that families should not be required to come to Mass because they are not exercising their free will, may be receiving Christ in a state of mortal sin or will be forever turned off to coming to Mass in the future. ***While yesteryear's parents wouldn't imagine not bringing their children to Mass, today, without a more direct prompting from the Church, very few parents have the faith or knowledge to be motivated to come to Mass.***

The National Catholic Reporter *published a survey citing* ***"Important Reasons for Not Going to Mass More Often."*** *The number one and two reasons among all generations of Catholics was:*[81]

1. **"I'm just not a religious person"**
2. **"Family responsibilities."**

This reveals families aren't necessarily opposed to the Mass itself. They just aren't motivated enough and therefore allow family activities to come first. How can a family be for or against the Mass if they are barely exposed to it?

"We know that they know."

As pointed out earlier in this book, despite the initial controversy in implementing a Mass/class program, the overwhelming majority of families stayed and came to Mass. However, it is interesting to consider what transpired at a nearby parish with parents in search of alternatives. Parents were forthcoming with the DRE in asking whether or not their child(ren) could attend class but not have to come to Mass. This was not about signing in for Mass. This was about not attending Mass on a regular basis.

This intent was also reflected in an on-line chat group:

> **"At ________ parish you are not required to go to Mass. They ask you to go but no one follows up so you really do not have to go to Mass."**

Naturally, this was a bit disconcerting to the parish. This attitude, however, isn't really shocking. As one DRE once told me, "We (DREs) have to stop acting surprised that religious education families no longer go to Mass." Nevertheless, important insights can be gleaned from considering the psychology of what is a typical scenario in parishes throughout this country. Parents are not oblivious to the fact that parish leaders know they are not coming to Mass. It is a type of unstated understanding… *"We know that they know"* that classroom attendance isn't optional, but Sunday Mass is. **It has gone on too long that parishes have indirectly "confirmed" students (and parents) in their choice of straying far from the authentic path to Jesus Christ through the Mass.**

Every organization, whether in business or sports, has core principles from which programs, processes, rules and regulations are built upon. To have faith formation without the Mass is akin to having a bank without money, a clothing store without clothes or learning to play baseball by reading a book. Faith formation programs must no longer exist without their core principle–Jesus Christ in and through the Mass. Along with any organization's core principles, such as school, work, or even extracurricular sports, is an accountability to those principles through one's presence and commitment. The Church has standards that are to be met before a person can receive a sacrament. The Church needs to reassess the only real measure by which readiness is determined, primarily class attendance. This was originally predicated on the assumption families were coming to Mass regularly, which is no longer the case. As is described in Chapter 2 (Confirmation & the Mass), and in accordance with Canon Law, Keeping the Lord's Day Holy is key in being "properly disposed". Accountability for being present at Mass, through a type of sign-in system, will go a long way in teaching and preparing students (and parents) for a more authentic journey with Christ and readiness for receiving the Sacraments.

In her book, *Forming Intentional Disciples: The Path to Knowing and Following Jesus*, Sherry Weddell completes an in-depth analysis of the Catholic culture in the United States. The statistics below are from 2007 but reflect generational differences that have led to a further decline in weekly Mass attendance rates as the "Builders" have aged. Below is the alarming survey and excerpt from her book:

Generation	Age	% Attending (Weekly Mass)
Builders	Ages 65+	45%
Boomers	Ages 47-64	20%
Gen X	Ages 26-46	13%
Millennials	**Ages 18-25**	**10%**

"Take a moment to consider the implications. More than 50% of Catholic adults are now GenXers or Millennials (18-25-year olds as of 2007). Both groups are teetering on the brink of single-digit weekly Mass attendance. **If younger Catholics are not going to Mass or getting married in the Church, why would they bother to raise their children in the faith?** We can no longer depend upon rites of passage or cultural, peer, or familial pressure to bring the majority back.

If this trend does not change, in ten years it will cease to matter that we have a priest shortage. The Builders (65+) will be largely gone, the Boomers retiring and our institutions, parishes and schools, will be emptying at an incredible rate."[82]

Further analysis of more recent data reveals a continuing downhill trend. The low weekly Mass attendance has decreased by 4.5% since 2005. Two polls (from CARA and Pew) show the number of Catholics has declined. There has also been a fairly dramatic decline in the number of primary age children enrolling in religious education by 38% in a fifteen-year span (especially considering the overall birth rate has only declined by close to 9.8%).[83] Additionally there has been a 90% increase in the number of former Catholic adults since 2005! The table below places these statistics and more in perspective:

Category	Year	Amount	Year	Amount	Change	Source
Weekly Mass Attendance All ages combined:	2005	25.6%	2019	21.1%	-4.5%	C.A.R.A. [84]
Catholic Population (Self-reported)	2005	81.2 million	2020	72.4 million	-8.8 million (-11%)	C.A.R.A. [84]
Number of US Catholics	2007	54.3 million	2014	50.9 million	-3 million	Pew[85]
Percentage of Catholics in US Population	2007	23.9%	2014	20.8%	-3.1%	Pew[85]
Percentage of Protestants in US Population	2007	51.3%	2014	46.5%	-4.8%	Pew[85]
Percentage of Unaffiliated (Atheist/Agnostic/Nothing) in US Population	2007	16.1%	2014	22.8%	**+6.7%**	Pew[85]
Primary School Children in US Religious Education	2005	3.4 million	2020	2.1 million	-1.3 million (-38%)	C.A.R.A. [84]
Former Catholic adults: Those raised Catholic who no longer self-identify as Catholic	2005	15.5 million	2020	29.5 million	+14 million +90%	C.A.R.A. [84]

According to another report, for every one Catholic convert, six more are leaving the Church.[86]

"LET THE CHILDREN COME TO ME"

Keeping in mind that many parents are loosely attached to the Church, within the context of a reasonable program parents are willing to be led to the Mass as has been demonstrated at St. Vincent de Paul Parish. Parents who sign their child for faith formation are not doing so because of societal pressures. There is no stigma in being raised without faith. In today's secular culture, parents deserve credit for caring enough to enroll their child(ren) in a faith formation program.

By signing up for a program, parents are entrusting the authority of church teaching to properly lead their children in the truths of the faith. While there is barely still time, the faith formation programs in the United States must seriously consider centering the entire program around the Mass as a necessary component. After all, God is the first to require us to 'Keep the Lord's Day Holy'.

It is at the Mass that one's free will is at least given a chance to embrace Christ in all his glorious fullness.

Many parishes, that used to have four Sunday morning Masses, now have only two or three. If all faith formation students were attending Mass every Sunday with their families, it most likely would become necessary to increase the number of Masses. What a blessing this would be!

11 Conclusion

The statistics are alarming and undeniable. Even with a slight rebound in 2025, weekly Mass attendance rates are unacceptably low. This combined with the incredible 90% increase in the number of former Catholic adults and a dramatic 38% decline in R.E. enrollment over the past fifteen years, traditional religious education programs have not and will not sustain the Catholic culture for much longer. Yet, faith formation is the main vehicle through which parents and their children can be reached.

The necessary paradigm shift in our country's faith formation has already begun with the acceptance and implementation of various forms of Family Faith or parental involvement in many parishes. The program at St. Vincent de Paul takes the concept of Family Faith a necessary, direct, and effective step closer to the heart of Catholicism, the Holy Mass, where parents are, in large measure, willing to be led. Participation in the Catholic spiritual pillars of our faith must become a primary component in faith formation and instead of competing with education, must collaborate with it. While the program described in this book is only in its foundational years, it is quickly showing progress. The feedback I have received from parishes that have implemented the program has been overwhelmingly positive. In presentations I give on this model, I describe it as a more holistic approach to faith formation compared to the traditional classroom model. First and foremost, it is grounded in the Eucharist. Parents are with their children at Mass, interact with them at Family Faith sessions, and participate with them in the prayer-filled spiritual pillars of the Church. Additionally, as a result of faith formation families' increased presence on Sundays, opportunities abound for greater integration into the parish community and ministries that welcome them with open arms.

Leaders of faith formation should not be afraid but rejoice in more directly leading families to the presence of Christ at Mass. He is longing to pour his grace on his children as they walk through the doors of His Church. He yearns to hear their hearts speak to Him, to ponder Him, to be healed by Him and to grow closer to experiencing Him in His fullness. Let us trust what Jesus can do.

A Final Note: As Your Parish Moves Forward

Some parishes that moved forward with a Mass-centered family faith formation, did so gradually, in steps, as we did at St. Vincent de Paul Parish. Others, convinced of the importance of the benefits of a Mass/class family-centered model, implemented the program in full immediately. I recommend beginning the program as shown on page 37 with a combination of classes and Family Faith sessions. Parish programs may have to be adjusted depending upon the number of students/families involved and space available. A two-hour time frame between Masses is ideal to make sure cars can easily enter and exit the premises.

Keep in mind the two most important aspects: Mass and family. The Holy Spirit will continue to move parishes more fervently towards the Mass and Eucharist, with children and parents beside each other. Begin by working out the logistics of bringing families to Mass. Then figure out how to fit in classes and Family Faith sessions around the Mass. I continue to try and balance an approach that is appealing to families while at the same time maintains Mass as the central aspect. May the Holy Spirit guide you in all you do!

12 References/Image Credits

1a. United States Conference of Catholic Bishops, *Directory for Catechesis,* Pontifical Council for the Promotion of the New Evangelization. Libreria Editrice Vaticana (LEV), Vatican City State, 2020, #227-231,9 5,9 6.

1b. *Directory for Catechesis* Vatican Liberia Editrice Vaticana, 2020, #96.

2. Sri, Edward. *A Biblical Walk Through the Mass*. Westchester, PA: Ascension Press, 2011, pg. 120 (Doxology at Mass).

3. Gray, Mark M. Editor. "Self-reported Mass Attendance of U.S. Catholics." The Center for Applied Research in the Apostolate, Georgetown University. Washington D.C. January 10, 2005. http://cara.georgetown.edu/attendpr.pdf (74% Mass Attendance in 1957-58).

Gray, Mark M. Editor. "Frequently Requested Church Statistics" Center for Applied Research in the Apostolate. Washington D.C.. 2017. http://cara.georgetown.edu/frequently-requested-church-statistics/

4a. Pope Benedict XVI , Angelus, June 26, 2011, Libreria Editrice Vaticana. https://www.vatican.va/content/benedict-xvi/en/angelus/2011/documents/hf_ben-xvi_ang_20110626.html

4b. United States Conference of Catholic Bishops, *National Directory for Catechesis*. USCCB, Washington, D.C.2 005, #33.

5a. *General Directory for Catechesis* Libreria Editrice Vaticana (LEV), Vatican City State, #51.

5b. *Directory for Catechesis,* #96.

6. Sherry Weddell, *Forming Intentional Disciples: The Path to Knowing and Following Jesus,* (Huntington, Indiana: Our Sunday Visitor, 2012).

7a. New Evangelization. United States Conference of Catholic Bishops 2017. http://www.usccb.org/beliefs-and-teachings/how-we-teach/new-evangelization/

7b. *Directory for Catechesis,* #426.

8a. *Directory for Catechesis,* #96.

8b. *National Directory for Catechesis,* #33.

9. *General Directory for Catechesis,* #51.

10a. *National Directory for Catechesis,* #4C.

10b. *Directory for Catechesis*, #95,9 6.

11. *General Directory for Catechesis,* #30.

12. *National Directory for Catechesis,* #33.

13. *General Directory for Catechesis,* #51.

14. *National Directory for Catechesis,* #33.

15. Szalavitz, Maia, "Touching Empathy." Psychology Today. March 1, 2010. https://www.psychologytoday.com/us/blog/born-love/201003/touching-empathy

16. *National Directory for Catechesis,* #19B.

17. *Catechism of the Catholic Church.* 2nd Ed. Vatican Liberia Editrice Vaticana, 2011, #1324, 1698.

18. United States Conference of Catholic Bishops. "Catechesis" 2020. http://www.usccb.org/beliefs-and-teachings/how-we-teach/catechesis/index.cfm

19. Cavins, Jeff. *I'm Not Being Fed*. Westchester, PA: Ascension Press, 2005, pg. 138.

20. *National Directory for Catechesis,* #34D, 43E.

21. *National Directory for Catechesis,* #61:4, 36:3a, 54C, 35D, 39.

22. Baptismal Promises, The English translation of *The Order of Baptism of Children* © 2017, International Commission on English in the Liturgy Corporation (ICEL); All rights reserved.

23. Glancey, Michael. "Confraternity of Christian Doctrine." *The Catholic Encyclopedia*. Vol. 3. New York: Robert Appleton Company, 1908. 26 Aug. 2019. http://www.newadvent.org/cathen/03711b.htm

24. *Ibid*. - New Advent.

25. St Pope Pius X, *Acerbo Nimis,On Teaching Christian Doctrine*" April 1905. http://w2.vatican.va/content/pius-x/en/encyclicals/documents/hf_p-x_enc_15041905_acerbo-nimis.html

26. *Ibid*. - *Acerbo Nimis.*

27. Armesen, Editor Routlege. *Encyclopedia of US Labor and Working Class History Volume 1.* Taylor & Francis Group, NY, NY 2007, page 698. https://books.google.com/

28. *Acerbo Nimis* - On Teaching Christian Doctrine, #7.

29. *General Directory for Catechesis,* #224.

30. *National Directory for Catechesis,* 17C.

31. *Ibid*. 17A.

32. Pope Paul VI, *Evangelii Nuntiandi-Evangelization in the Modern World* Dec. 8, 1975 #28. http://www.vatican.va/content/paul-vi/en/apost_exhortations/documents/hf_p-vi_exh_19751208_evangelii-nuntiandi.html

33. *National Directory for Catechesis*, 17C.

34. *Ibid. 17C.*

35. *Ibid. 17A.*

36. *Ibid*.17D.

37. *Ibid*.17D.

38. *Ibid*.17E.

39. International Council for Catechesis, "Adult Catechesis in the Christian Community" St. Paul Publications, 1990. #66. http://www.vatican.va/roman_curia/congregations/cclergy/documents/rc_con_cclergy_doc_14041990_acat_en.html

40. *General Directory for Catechesis*, #3

41. Lewinski, Ronald J. *An Introduction to the RCIA*. Archdiocese of Chicago; Liturgy Training Publications, Chicago, IL, Loc.1622 (Glossary).

42. The English translation of *The Order of Christian Initiation of Adults* © 2018 International Commission on English in the Liturgy Corporation (ICEL). All rights reserved.

43. *Ibid*. *OCIA*, #47, #79.

44. O'Neil, Megan, "Lack of funding causes lay-run RCIA ministry organization to dissolve" National Catholic Register. May 8, 2013. https://www.ncronline.org/news/parish/lack-funding-causes-lay-run-rcia-ministry-organization-dissolve

North American Forum on the Catechumenate, Washington DC. May 17, 2013; https://romancatholicworld.files.wordpress.com/2013/05/rcia-the-north-american-forum-on-the-catechum; https://fdlc.org/content/grants-preserve-legacy-north-american-forum

45. Thomas H. Morris, *The RCIA: Transforming the Church, A Resource for Pastoral Implementation* (Mahwah, New Jersey: Paulist Press, 1989), (Three Basic Principles from the Rite).

46. *OCIA*, #83.

47. *The RCIA: Transforming the Church*, Loc. 684 (Begin with the End in Mind).

48. Steven R. Covey, *The 7 Habits of Highly Effective People* (New York: Simon and Schuster, 2020). https://www.franklincovey.com/the-7-habits/habit-2.html

49. Pope Paul VI, *Sacrosanctum Concilium* – Constitution on the Sacred Liturgy, Dec 4, 1963, #10. https://www.vatican.va/archive/hist_councils/ii_vatican_council/documents/vat-ii_const_19631204_sacrosanctum-concilium_en.html

50. USCCB (United States Conference of Catholic Bishops), "Sing to the Lord: Music in Divine Worship." Nov 14, 2007, #9.

51. The *RCIA, Transforming the Church,* Loc. 693 (Begin with the End in Mind).

52. *Ibid*. Loc. 455 (Ritual Prayer).

53. Father Ronald Lewinski, (1946-2017) Co-director of the Department of Parish Vitality and Mission for the Archdiocese of Chicago; http://www.usccb.org/about/divine-worship/newsletter/upload/newsletter-2014-10.pdf; https://www.archchicago.org/obituary/-/article/2017/07/24/archdiocesan-priest-rev-ronald-john-lewinski-dies ; https://archny.org/the-rcia-we-know-about-it-heres-a-chance-to-know-more/

54. Ronald J. Lewinski, *An Introduction to the RCIA: The Vision of Christian Initiation,* Chicago: Liturgy Training Publications, 2017.

55. *Sacrosanctum Concilium,* General Norms for the Liturgical Year, #102. https://www.vatican.va/archive/hist_councils/ii_vatican_council/documents/vat-ii_const_19631204_sacrosanctum-concilium_en.html

56. GNLYC, *General Norms for the Liturgical Year and the Calendar*. Congregation for Divine Worship., Feb 14, 1969, #17, 43; https://www.ewtn.com/catholicism/library/liturgical-year-2193

57. *Catechism of the Catholic Church,* #2180, 2186.

58. *National Directory for Catechesis,* #19.

59. *The RCIA, Transforming the Church*. Loc. 475.

60a. *Catechism of the Catholic Church*, #1309).

60b. The Canon Law Society,*The Canon Law Letter & Spirit*, The Liturgical Press, Collegeville, Minnesota, 1995, #1750.

61. Grondin, Father Charles, "When Can Confirmation be Denied?" Catholic Answers. https://www.catholic.com/qa/when-can-confirmation-be-denied

62. Kowalska, Blessed Sister M. Faustina Catholic Church. *Diary, Divine Mercy in My Soul*. Association of Marian Helpers, Stockbridge, MA 1999, #1811, 1447.

63. LaBanca, Nicholas. "The Blood of the Martyrs." Ascension Press. 9/17/18. https://media.ascensionpress.com/2018/09/17/blood-of-the-martyrs-is-still-seed-for-the-church/

64a. Synod of Bishops, XIII Ordinary General Assembly. "The New Evangelization for the Transmission of the Christian Faith – Instrumentum Laboris." Vatican City 2012, #46; http://www.vatican.va/roman_curia/synod/documents/rc_synod_doc_20120619_instrumentum-xiii_en.html #46.

64b. Padre Pio. https://www.padrepiodapietrelcina.com/en/quotes-of-padre-pio-padre-pios-words-of-faith/

65. Gray, Mark M. Editor. "Frequently Requested Church Statistics" Center for Applied Research in the Apostolate. Washington D.C.. 2017. http://cara.georgetown.edu/frequently-requested-church-statistics/

66. Smith, Gregory A.. "Just one-third of U.S. Catholic agree with their church that Eucharist is body, blood of Christ" Pew Research Center, August 5, 2019. (31% real presence); https://www.pewresearch.org/fact-tank/2019/08/05/transubstantiation-eucharist-u-s-catholics/

67. 2015 Survey of U.S. Catholics and Family Life https://www.pewresearch.org/religion/2015/09/02/chapter-2-participation-in-catholic-rites-and-observances/ (60% Confession statistic).

68. *Forming Intentional Disciples*. (80% Confirmation statistic)

69. Gray, Mark M. Editor. "Self-reported Mass Attendance of U.S. Catholics." The Center for Applied Research in the Apostolate, Georgetown University. Washington D.C. January 10, 2005. http://cara.georgetown.edu/attendpr.pdf (74% Mass Attendance in 1957)

70. Bourbon, Julie. "Study Asks: Why are young Catholics, going, going gone." 1/22/2018. National Catholic Reporter Publishing Company, Kansas. https://www.ncronline.org/news/parish/study-asks-why-are-young-catholics-going-going-gone

71a. *General Directory for Catechesis*, #59.

71b. Smith, Christian and Adamczyk, Amy. Handing Down the Faith. Oxford Univ. Press. 2021), pg. 35 *(Other religions included in study were Mormon, Hindu and Buddhist).*

72a. *General Directory for Catechesis*, #226.

72b. Smith, Christian and Adamczyk, Amy. *Handing Down the Faith*. Oxford Univ. Press. 2021), pg. 7 *(Religions included were Catholic, Protestant, Jewish, Mormon, Muslim, Hindu and Buddhist).*

72c. *General Directory for Catechesis*, #226, 227.

72d. *Directory for Catechesis*, #227-31.

72e. *Ibid*. #124.

72f. *Ibid*. #232.

73a. Saint Pope John Paul II, "*Rosarium Virginis Mariae*" Vatican: The Holy See. Rome. Oct. 15, 2002.; https://w2.vatican.va/content/john-paul-ii/en/apost_letters/2002/documents/hf_jp-ii_apl_20021016_rosarium-virginis-mariae.html

73b. Saint Louis De Montfort. *The Secret of the Rosary*. Montfort Publication, NY. 1995 pg. 18.

73c. Beebe, Catherine. *Saint Dominic and the Rosary*. Ignatius Press, San Francisco. 1984, pg. 91.

74. Saint Pope John Paul II, "*Rosarium Virginis Mariae*" Vatican: The Holy See. Rome. Oct. 15, 2002.; https://w2.vatican.va/content/john-paul-ii/en/apost_letters/2002/documents/hf_jp-ii_apl_20021016_rosarium-virginis-mariae.html

75a. Saint Pope John Paul II, "Letter of Holy Father John Paul II to the Bishop of Liege, Mgr. Albet Houssiau on the Occasion of the 750th Anniversary of the Festival of the '*Corpus Domini*'" 1996. http://w2.vatican.va/content/john-paul-ii/fr/letters/1996/documents/hf_jp-ii_let_19960528_corpus-domini.html

75b. Gray, Mark M. Editor. "The Sacrament of Reconciliation" Center for Applied Research in the Apostolate. Washington, D.C. Feb. 2008. http://cara.georgetown.edu/reconciliation.pdf (75% Confession statistic)

76. Kowalska, Blessed Sister M. Faustina Catholic Church. Diary, *Divine Mercy in My Soul*. Association of Marian Helpers, Stockbridge, MA. 1999, #699.

77. Digest of Education Statistics. "Average daily attendance (ADA) as a percentage of total enrollment, school day length, and school year length in public schools, by school level and state: 2003-04 and 2007-08." NCES -N ational Center for Education Statistics. June 2011. https://nces.ed.gov/programs/digest/d11/tables/dt11_043.asp

78. Tugend, Alina. "Praise is fleeting but Brickbats We Recall" The New York Times 2017. http://www.nytimes.com/2012/03/24/your-money/why-people-remember-negative-events-more-than-positive-ones.html

79. Blackshaw, Pete. *Satisfied Customers Tell Three Friends. Angry Customers Tell 3,000*. Random House, Inc. NY, 2008.

80a. Pew Research Center. "One in Five US Adults were Raise in Inter Faith Homes" Pew Forum on Religion and Public Life, Washington, DC. 10/26/2016. https://www.pewresearch.org/religion/2016/10/26/one-in-five-u-s-adults-were-raised-in-interfaith-homes/

80b. Ibid. "One in Five US Adults were Raise in Inter Faith Homes" Pew Forum on Religion and Public Life, Washington, DC. 3/22/2016. https://www.pewresearch.org/religion/2016/03/22/gender-differences-in-worship-attendance-vary-across-religious-groups/

80c. *Handing Down the Faith*, pg. 5.

80d. *Directory for Catechesis*. #124.

80e. Shawn Achor, *The Happiness Advantage: How a Positive Brain Fuels Success in Work and Life* (New York: Random House, 2010), pp. 146-148.

81. D'Antonio, William. "Survey Reveals Generation Shift in the Catholic Church" 10/12/2011. National Catholic Reporter Publishing Company, Kansas. https://www.ncronline.org/news/survey-reveals-generation-shift-catholic-church

82. *Forming Intentional Disciples*, pp. 38-39. (Attending Sunday Mass)

83. "Number of births in the United States from 1990 to 2016 (in millions)." Statistica, Inc., NY. 2018; https://www.statista.com/statistics/195908/number-of-births-in-the-united-states-since-1990/

84. Gray, Mark M. Editor. "Frequently Requested Church Statistics" Center for Applied Research in the Apostolate. Washington, D.C.. 2017. http://cara.georgetown.edu/frequently-requested-church-statistics/

85. Pew Research Center. "America's Changing Religious Landscape" Pew Forum on Religion and Public Life, Washington, DC. 5/12/2015. http://www.pewforum.org/2015/05/12/americas-changing-religious-landscape/

86. McLoughlin, Michael. "Pew Survey: Percentage of US Catholics drops and Catholicism is losing members faster than any Denomination." Crux Catholic Media Inc., 5/12/2015.; https://cruxnow.com/church/2015/05/12/pew-survey-percentage-of-us-catholics-drops-and-catholicism-is-losing-members-faster-than-any-denomination/

Image Credits

Cover Images: Monart Design/stock.adobe.com; Fabio Lotti/stock.adobe.com; Rawpixel.com/stock.adobe.com; **Cover Art:** korkeng/stock.adobe.com; **page 18:** Rawpixel.com/stock.adobe.com; **page 20:** Tomsickov/stock.adobe.com; **page 24:** Godong Photo/stock.adobe.com; **page 28:** CIRIC/Bayard; **page 33:** muratart/stock.adobe.com, CIRIC/Bayard; **page 36:** isara/stock.adobe.com; **page 38:** CIRIC/Bayard; **page 39:** (c) *The Beacon*, Diocese of Paterson, NJ. Used with Permission., StockPhotosArt /stock.adobe.com, CIRIC/Bayard; **page 41:** Adam Ján Figel'/stock.adobe.com; **page 42:** Chris/stock.adobe.com; **page 43:** Bayard, Inc.; **page 44:** Emanuele Capoferri/stock.adobe.com; **page 45:** GISTEL/stock.adobe.com; **page 46:** Monkey Business/stock. Deirdre Nemeth; **page 48:** PR Image Factory/stock.adobe.com; **page 51:** Deirdre Nemeth; **page 53:** Donna Cubelli; **page 54:** Donna Cubelli; **page 55:** Syda Production/stock.adobe.Deirdre Nemeth; **page 62:** Allistair/peopleimages.com/stock.adobe.com; **page 63:** PhotoGranary/stock.adobe.com; **page 66:** highwaystarz/stock.adobe.com; **page 70:** Deirdre Nemeth; **page 73:** Rawpixel.com/stock.adobe.com; **page 79:** CIRIC/Bayard; **page 81:** Rawpixel.com/stock.adobe.com ; **page 91-92:** © *The Beacon*, Diocese of Paterson, NJ. Used with Permission.

THE BEACON
JUNE 13, 2019
THE AWARD-WINNING NEWSPAPER OF THE R.C. DIOCESE OF PATERSON, N.J.

SIXTH ANNUAL CORPUS CHRISTI FOOD DRIVE

Faithful asked to donate food for Catholic Charities food pantries

By CECILE PAGLIARULO
REPORTER

PATERSON A client walks through the aisles of the Father English Food Pantry here, selecting the food items she needs to feed her family. She places them in shopping bags with the words "thank you" printed on them in bright red lettering. For each and every client, there are endless "thank you" moments with more than 25,000 visits each year by the needy, making the Catholic Charities food pantries some of the busiest in the state.

As the summer approaches, Bishop Serratelli is reaching out to all Catholics in the Diocese to help those in need by donating food to the sixth annual Corpus Christi Food Drive at weekend Masses June 22 and 23. The summer months are a critical time for food donations to pantries because it was a time when the shelves are empty with fewer donations coming in to Catholic Charities, which relies heavily on the generosity of parishes and schools.

> **"Catholic Charities is one of the most important local sources of food for literally thousands of our brothers and sisters in genuine need — particularly children."**
>
> – BISHOP SERRATELLI

"We are getting close to our biggest food drive of the year and we are very excited for this wonderful event since the number of clients we serve continues to grow," said Carlos Roldan, director of Catholic Charities food pantries. "The faithful across the Diocese help us feed so many in need."

The Corpus Christi Food Drive was created in 2014 to alleviate the food shortage problem that occurred during the summer. According to Roldan, in addition to fewer food donations coming in during the summer, children, who are off from school for summer vacation, do not have their regular meal at school. For many of the chil-

FOOD DRIVE ON **6**

BEACON PHOTO | JOE GIGLI

HONORED JUBILARIANS Bishop Serratelli served as the main celebrant of the Diocese's annual Priests Jubilee Mass June 4 in St. Patrick Church in Chatham to mark milestone ordination anniversaries — 25, 40, 50 and 60 years — of 16 priests who serve or have served the Church of Paterson. He is pictured after the liturgy with the jubilarians who were concelebrants (top row, from left): Msgr. John Wehrlen, 60 years; Father John Hanley, 25 years; Franciscan Father of the Renewal Terry Messer, 25 years; and Jesuit Father Kirk Reynolds, 40 years; (bottom row, from left): Trinitarian Father Ralph Frisch, 60 years; Father Brendan Murray, 50 years; and Msgr. Kevin Flanagan, 60 years. Father Murray delivered the homily during the Mass. See story and more photos on pages 10-11.

Family formation program, 'I Am the Way, the Truth and the Life,' taking root in parishes

By MICHAEL WOJCIK
NEWS EDITOR

STIRLING A movement in religious education started to take root last year in several parishes of the Diocese with the new Family Faith Formation Program, developed by a local parish religious education director, that helps entire families center their lives around their faith and the summit of our faith: the Mass. Endorsed by Bishop Serratelli, the initiative encourages parents and children to attend Mass together; learn more about their faith, both together and in age-appropriate settings; and share their faith with each other.

Still in its infancy, Family Faith Formation, developed by Deidre Nemeth, religious education director of St. Vincent de Paul Parish here, suggests that parish religious education programs adopt six "spiritual pillars" that re-orient religious formation from only classroom teaching to instruction of the faith centered around the Mass that includes teaching entire families, both children and their parents. Already, the program — part of a larger national Family Faith Formation movement — has started to bare spiritual fruit in the six local parishes, which piloted it in the Diocese, said Nemeth. Last year, she wrote a 42-page booklet that outlines the initiative, "I Am the Way, the Truth and the Life: a Family Formation Program for the New Evangelization," available now to parishes.

These participating parishes have reported increases in both parents and children growing in "learning and sacramentally living" their faith by attending religious education classes that give them a greater understanding of the Mass, especially the Eucharist; attending Mass more regularly; practicing their faith more at home; and forging a stronger relationship with their parish, including a greater willingness to volunteer,

'I AM THE WAY' ON **8**

Appendix

THE BEACON ARTICLE CONTINUED

'I Am the Way': Family formation program taking root in diocesan parishes

FROM **1**

Nemeth writes in the booklet, which features a forward by Bishop Serratelli.

"The program connects families to the Mass by leading them to attend Mass every week. We want to make a big statement: that the Mass, especially the Eucharist — the source and summit of our faith — is important. We have found that there is a greater openness of families to come to Mass — and participating in Adoration, rosary and confession — than we first realized," said Nemeth, who began developing Family Faith Formation at Our Lady of Mount Carmel Parish (OLMC), Boonton, where she started serving as director of religious education in 2011 under Father Richard Carton, then pastor. In 2015, she continued to hone and expand the program, when she became religious education director at St. Vincent's, again under Father Carton's leadership as pastor. "This program gives great hope for the future of the Catholic faith," she said.

Over the 2018-19 academic year, the following four parishes of the Diocese joined OLMC and St. Vincent's in implementing Family Faith Formation: the Cathedral of St. John the Baptist, Paterson; St. Michael's, Netcong; St. Kateri Tekakwitha, Sparta; and St. Catherine of Siena, Mountain Lakes. In the booklet, published by the Diocese, Nemeth suggests that parishes reduce the length of their religion classes to about 30 to 40 minutes and schedule them on Sundays before or after Masses. While the parents wait for their children, parishes should offer religious formation to the adults in the form of a class, a speaker, a DVD series or an opportunity for fellowship. Twice each year, parishes can schedule Family Faith Sessions — two-hour sessions that offer instruction and activities that engage participants of all ages — often together — on a variety of topics, usually during Advent and Lent, writes Nemeth, who is also president of the diocesan Catechetical Leaders Association.

In the booklet, Nemeth suggests that parishes introduce the following six "spiritual pillars" to their religious instruction:

- **Mass** — attended as a family each Sunday.
- **Rosary** — prayed in its entirety by families as a parish once a year and prayed a decade at a time before Masses.
- **Eucharistic Adoration** — involving families, who gather to adore Christ in the Eucharist once each year.
- **Confession** — with families scheduled to come once per year, during Lent.
- **Stations of the Cross** — attended by families, during Lent.
- **Divine Mercy Sunday** — gathering families in Divine Mercy parish prayers on the Sunday after Easter.

In the booklet, Nemeth writes, "Participation in the spiritual pillars is bringing parents directly in touch with our living God. Even souls, not previously interested, must perceive this at some level and are opening up to the effects of this grace." She also emphasizes that parishes can adopt any number of the "spiritual pillars." Last year, Nemeth promoted Family Faith Formation around the Diocese, encouraged by an enthusiastic Bishop Serratelli.

> **"This program has made a huge impact at St. John's. Families are more enthusiastic about coming to Mass together and sharing their faith at home."**
>
> — IVANNIA VEGA-MCTIGHE

In the booklet's forward, Bishop Serratelli writes, "In a time when there are many challenges to the Church's mission of catechesis ... Deirdre Nemeth's approach ... is one of the most successful new approaches of our times."

"Her approach of family faith formation not only recognizes this reality, but also helps the parents both grow in their own faith and in their responsibility of bringing up the children in the Catholic faith. Anyone who adopts this method of catechesis cannot help but see positive results," Bishop

teaching, better behavior exhibited by the students and greater desire to volunteer among parents and children. Because the class sessions have been cut from 90 minutes down to 30 or 40 minutes each, some parishes schedule a greater number of sessions in an academic year, said Nemeth, also inspired to develop the initiative locally after attending a 2011 conference of the Center for Ministry Development in Florida.

For the Family Faith Sessions, curriculum should be based on themes from the Catechism and the Catholic Church, such as the profession of faith, liturgy and the sacraments, morality and Christian prayer. These sessions should include an all-ages learning experience, an in-depth learning experience and ways to apply these lessons at home. At St. Vincent's, many parents at first questioned whether the sessions would be worth their time in their busy lives but after, told Nemeth that they "enjoyed discussing the faith with their children."

In the booklet, Father Carton writes, "In this program, parents, who often feel inadequate in teaching the faith, and parish directors of faith formation programs are drawn together to create something beautiful. Children and parents, side by side, learning and growing in faith is a beautiful gift for all involved." He also acknowledged, "With change, programs sometimes meet resistance. However, we are aware that the former classroom model that has been used is not effective and it is a Spirit-driven move to try that, which is new."

At St. John's, Ivannia Vega-McTighe, diocesan assistant director of evangelization; Sylvia Ortiz, the cathedral's coordinator of catechesis; and its catechetical team implemented Family Faith Formation last September with support from Msgr. Geno Sylva, St. John's rector and diocesan vicar for special projects. Now, more families attend Mass together and are eager to volunteer in the parish. After Masses, families walk to the cathedral center, where children receive the classroom portion of faith formation, while adults also receive a teaching from priests. Families also participate in monthly at-home projects — one asked them what they were thankful for — and joined together at the center last December for a Christmas celebration, she said.

"This program has made a huge impact at St. John's. Families are more enthusiastic about coming to Mass together and sharing their faith at home. They also are building relationships with our priests and each other," Vega-McTighe said. "We want to give families time to fall in love with the Eucharist — the key to every Catholic's life. Our catechists see our parents as partners — as the most important part of their children's faith formation," she said.

SCRIPTURE SEARCH®

Scriptures for June 16, 2019
Romans 5:1-5 and John 16:12-15

Following is a word search based on the Second Reading and reading for the feast of the Most Holy Trinity, Cycle C. The words can be found in all directions in the puzzle.

JUSTIFIED	BY FAITH	PEACE
LORD	JESUS	GAINED
ACCESS	GRACE	WE STAND
HOPE	GLORY OF GOD	PRODUCES
CHARACTER	LOVE	SPIRIT
CANNOT BEAR	TRUTH	GUIDE YOU
SPEAK	WHAT IS	DECLARE

JUSTIFIED

H O B Y F A I T H O P E
C A N N O T B E A R R C
D W C R E T C A R A H C
O E E C A R G K L W S T
G S I L E O H C R E I R
F T W F G S E D C R M U
O A H C I D S U I E E T
Y N A J E T D P V P R H
R D T N O O S O E E L A
O J I D R O L U Y A O N
L A S P S U S E J C K A
G U I D E Y O U F E R N

Notes

Notes

Notes

Notes

Notes

Notes